Thinking About Cities

New Perspectives on Urban Problems

Anthony H. Pascal, Editor

The Rand Corporation

Dickenson Publishing Company, Inc.
Belmont, California

Library of Congress Catalog Card Number: 78–106505

Printed in the United States of America

Contents

III. The Reform of Urban Programs 81

IV. Urban Violence and Public Order 139

Preface

Voicing concern about cities is a popular pastime in contemporary America. People seem to do a lot more musing, wondering, and speculating about cities, for example, than they ever did about the American frontier in its heyday. Television documentaries, Sunday supplement articles, and magazine features —which tend to have somewhere in their titles such words as urban, crisis, metropolitan, or problems—of course stimulate a good deal of the mental and vocal activity expressing the concern. It can be argued, however, that what the Urban (Metropolitan) Crisis (Problem) has not generated sufficiently is thinking. This volume is an attempt to remedy the lack. In it fifteen writers express thoughts about cities and about the problems cities manifest. Their backgrounds are diverse: seven are economists, three are sociologists, two are journalists, one is a city planner, one a psychiatrist, and one a political scientist. Each has attempted to apply the tools of his craft or the insights gained from his special knowledge to improve understanding of the metropolis as a stage on which the social, political, and economic drama is acted out. Their thinking is also brought to bear on the development of ways to improve the performance.

These papers were originally presented at the Workshop on Urban Programs held at The Rand Corporation in 1967–68. The workshop, organized in response to the initiation of research by Rand for the city of New York, the Office of Economic Opportunity, and the Department of Housing and Urban Development, was jointly sponsored by Rand and the Ford

Foundation. The Foundation's assistance in making possible the conference and thus in the assembling of these papers for publication here is gratefully acknowledged.

The purpose of the workshop was to help form and launch a comprehensive, long-term research program within Rand on urban policy issues and to stimulate other organizations to engage in related work. The intention was not only to generate ideas for particular programs but also to develop a larger structure for the continuing analysis and evaluation of urban problems.

A number of the participants drafted papers containing recommendations for program initiatives, research, and experiments in the following program areas: education, health services, welfare/public assistance, jobs and manpower training, housing and urban planning, police services and public order, and municipal finance and administration. In addition, papers were invited on issues cutting across program lines but of sufficient independent importance to warrant separate treatment. For example, participants wrote on such themes as race relations, bureaucracy, governmental decentralization, metropolitanization, municipal objectives, and the role of the private sector.

This book contains a selection of these invited papers.[1] Though they vary in depth of treatment and degree of definitiveness—some being historical, others analytical, and still others hortatory—they present a wide array of perspectives on America's urban problems. The papers fall into four groups.

The first two papers examine the city as the new focal point for contacts between blacks and whites. Earl Raab, for example, concentrates explicitly on the connection between urban problems and the situation of black Americans. By comparing the current situation of blacks with the historical situations of other ethnic groups in America, he assesses the prospects for the emergence of Negroes into the American mainstream. Alvin Poussaint analyzes the effects of slavery, Reconstruction, Jim Crow, and the ghetto on the black psyche, and discusses the

[1] A related Rand Memorandum entitled *Cities in Trouble: An Agenda for Urban Research* (RM-5603-RC, August 1968) is also available. It represents a synthesis of workshop findings as developed by a group of Rand authors. In it, I. S. Lowry writes on housing, A. H. Pascal on manpower training and jobs, D. M. Weiler on education, W. A. Johnson and R. Rosencranz on welfare, D. F. Loveday and S. M. Genensky on public order and the police, and C. T. Whitehead on health care.

implications of racism and poverty for urban planning and social action.

The papers in the next group concern themselves with the analysis and structuring of municipal goals, functions, and methods of organization, and the ways in which city governments should be programmed to face complex problems. Robert Dorfman asks what functions the city performs and how conflicts among the functions identified may be resolved. He points out some avenues for attaining better coordination in making cities work effectively. Kenneth Arrow reviews the bases of planning decisions by municipal authorities and discusses the ways by which more valid choice criteria may be inserted into this process. A conceptual analysis of decentralization and its meaning in the municipal sphere is the subject of the paper by Julius Margolis. In it he writes about the interrelationships among decentralization and political values, administrative efficiency, externalities, incentives, and information. Irving Kristol sounds a warning against the current fascination with decentralization of governmental functions and points to some of the benefits of bureaucracy which tend to be ignored.

The theme of the third group of papers is urban services, with particular emphasis on those programs designed to alleviate poverty and to rehabilitate the poor. The section begins with my own eight proposals for more market-oriented, voluntaristic approaches to these goals. Lester Thurow reviews current manpower and skill training programs. He notes how their defects are the result of systematic failures, which leads him to recommend new kinds of programs based on the restructuring of incentives. Stephen Enke advocates a much larger commitment to family planning services as an aid to the poor and as a way to reduce poverty. His calculations reveal that birth control programs, which seem to be widely desired by poor women, are apt to have impressive benefit-cost ratios. A survey of recent attitudes about welfare—their genesis, validation, and current status—is the main concern of Nathan Glazer's paper. He identifies the continuing gaps in knowledge which inhibit significant reforms in the important field of public assistance. Edward Logue discusses the distribution of services among the various constituent parts of the metropolis. He sees inequality in service provision as a primary defect of the current system and sketches a method for gauging inequities. The group concludes with a paper by Burton Weisbrod on the interplay between the goals of efficiency and equity in the design and operation of human service programs in the city.

With the fourth group of papers, race reemerges as a specific concern, for in it are discussed various aspects of urban violence and public order. Seymour Martin Lipset traces the historical role of violence in American cities. He analyzes the socioeconomic roots of the propensity to engage in extremist political action and how these extremist tendencies lead to public disorder. Guy Pauker presents some parallels between black dissatisfactions in the United States and the independence movements in colonial areas. He believes that the return of the black veteran from Vietnam presents the country with both a challenge and an opportunity and must receive special attention. The part played by the news media in informing us about the urban crisis is the subject of Ben Bagdikian's paper. He proposes a strategy for the media to follow in these uncertain times which will help them preserve their commitments both to objective truth and to necessary reform.

A striking fact emerges from a perusal of these contributions; when fifteen experienced observers are asked to think about cities, they all deal to a greater or lesser degree with the problems of race, of poverty, of equality, and of social harmony or its absence. Neither taxes, nor transit, neither public employees' strikes, nor the esthetics of urban renewal are seen as the central problem. The future of cities as places where people cluster to work out their joint destinies and the concern about whether these processes generate amenity and civility or squalor and strife is taken to be the central problem. To an extent, then, this book reflects the current predilection to use "urban problems" as a euphemism for the problems of race and poverty which are most starkly visible in the cities. Apologies, possibly, are in order for the adoption of a euphemism; no apology is required, I would maintain, for the emphasis expressed here.

Anthony H. Pascal
Santa Monica, California

Thinking About Cities

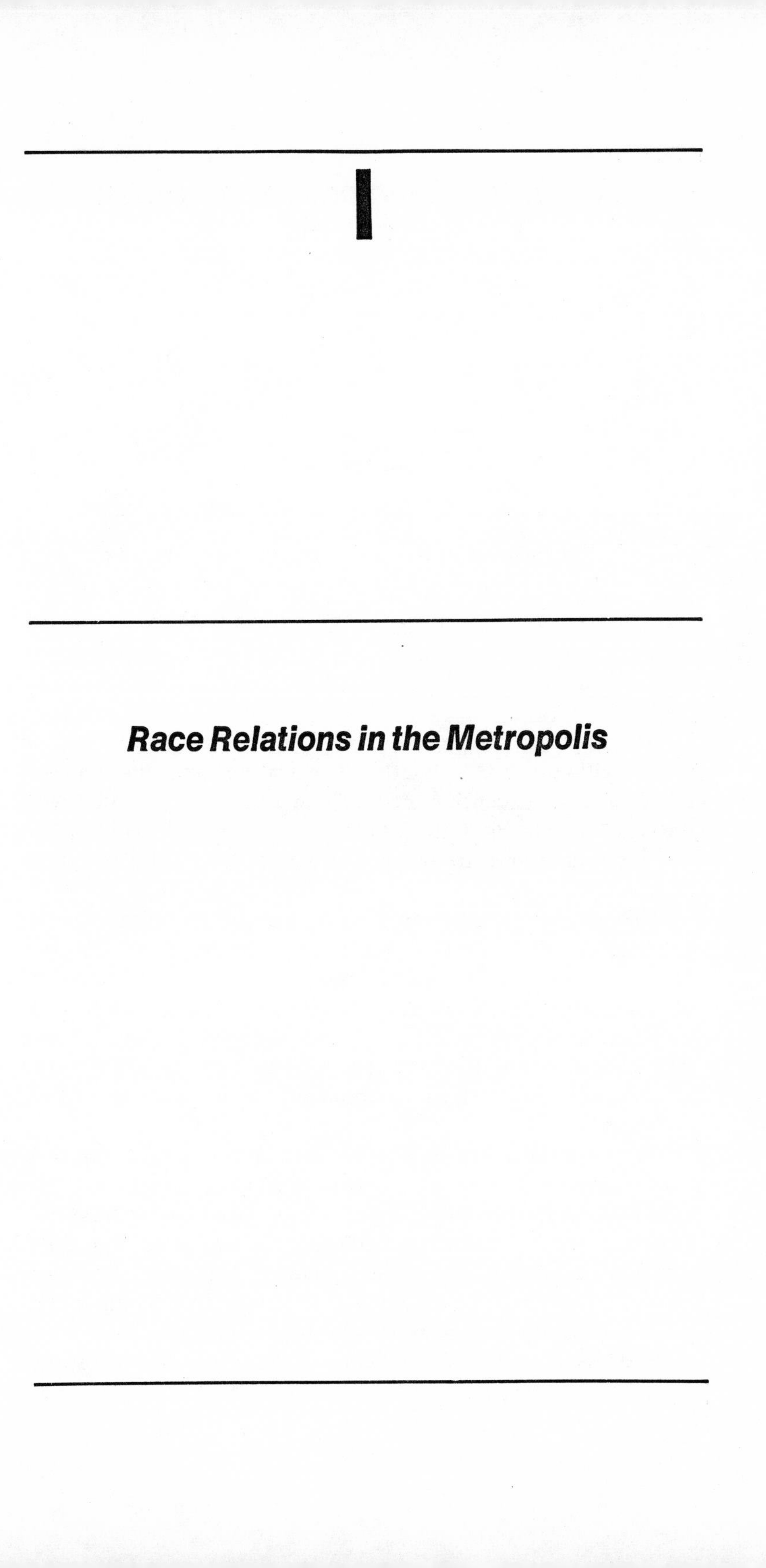

I

Race Relations in the Metropolis

A Renewed Perspective on Urban Problems

Earl Raab

San Francisco Jewish Community Relations Council

"The appalling thing about war," said Georg Brandes," is that it kills all love of truth." The war on and about urban problems is no exception. Few people who are acquainted with the truth are saying quite what they mean. Programs of action and research about urban problems have largely fallen out of perspective.

It should be clear to start with that the "problems of the city" today are really the problems of the Negro in the city. There are, of course, various Spanish-speaking counterparts here and there, but the Negroes can stand as the archetypal problem. Problems of housing, employment, welfare, crime, and education could all be dealt with if there weren't the Negro dimension. Indeed, so could problems of traffic and air pollution.

The initial question is whether this is a new problem, or a familiar old American problem with new complications. We have had constantly emerging ethnic populations in the cities, for example, the Irish, the Italians, and the Jews. Typically, they have emerged from abject poverty. Typically, they have emerged from crime-producing, dependency-producing ethnically segregated urban slum ghettoes. Typically, they have emerged from a state of low skill and low education. Typically, they have been a scandal and a threat to the older populations of the cities.

Now, we have a new mass migration to the cities: the Negroes, whom a perverted history is finally bringing to a state of emergence. The special complications that exist for this new population, as against the others, are obvious enough. For example:

1) Color is more difficult to overcome than ethnos—in the initial bars of discrimination, and in the latter processes of cultural merger.
2) The economy is a more difficult one into which to emerge. In the older eras it was more possible to move into the economy with lower skills and lower education. (In 1900, about 20 percent of the nonfarm jobs were unskilled, in 1950 about 8 percent. In 1900 about 6 percent of the American population were high school graduates; in 1950 about 60 percent).

But both of these complications are matters of degree. There are enough indications that color *qua* color can fade as a factor in America. Negro college graduates can now compete with white college graduates on the larger job markets. The white daughters of upper-class Brahmins are about as likely to marry Negroes today as they were to marry second generation Sicilians at the turn of the century.

And the differential problem of entering the economy is something less—or different—than it seems at first glance. There are fewer unskilled jobs by far in a manual training sense, but the number of service and white collar jobs which really require no specific skills or parental traditions is increasing. On the face of it, the economy is not that much more impenetrable for the 25-year-old Negro population in the city today, given its pattern of capabilities, than it was for the 25-year-old immigrant population a half century ago.

Black Attributes

But there are other complicating differences between the two immigrant eras having to do not with white attitudes or the economy, but with the developed stance, and mood, of the Negro community itself. First of all, there may be much correspondence between the problems of the Negro immigrant population in the cities today and those of the older ethnic immigration populations; but, on another level, it is specious to call them both immigrant populations. Negroes are old Americans, sixth-generation Americans. First- and second-generation Italian, Irish, and Jewish immigrants imported their depressed state from Europe, and could only blame Europe. Negroes, as far as memory wanders, were deliberately and artificially depressed by America, and can only blame America. Indeed in the last 20 years, the official American society has repeatedly and unprecedentedly proclaimed its own guilt. There wasn't Irish Anger (at least, not at America), or Italian or Jewish Anger. There is Black Anger.

There is also, uniquely, Black Pessimism. The old immigrants came hopefully from hopeless societies looking for gold in the American streets. It took a backbreaking generation or two, but they found it. Negroes have awakened sharply to the fact that they have lived in a highly mobile society for longer than anyone, and they haven't seemed to do much moving. They are wary about high expectations.

There is something else, even less tangible: The old immigrants moved from one system into another. They had been depressed but not so alienated in the Old Country, where rigid economic and social stratification was normative. In their own fashion, they had been part of that system. They came to America, and, living on their cultural capital, were a restless interim population until they entered the American system on one acceptable level or another. But the Negroes, Americans only, were embedded in an American subsystem for generations without any sense of having an interim status preparatory to entering the main American system. There developed a *stable* Black Isolation, cultural and intellectual, of a kind ethnic immigrants didn't experience.

These black attributes have created time-bearing complications. They depress motivation and educational standards. They probably have a specific relationship to job entry. Perhaps the job market of the 1900s and that of the 1960s are not differentiated as much by the new requirement for skilled workers as by the new requirement for socialized and acculturated workers. Employers of the 1900s were receptive to deviant immigrant language, habits, clothing, and mien, partly because of their ultimate reliance on the immigrant labor market, partly because of the kinds of jobs, partly because of the kinds of expectations they had, and partly because they had not yet invented personnel officers and testing procedures. In this sense, because of their longtime isolation, a segment of the Negro population is "immigrant" in their deviant cultural characteristics of language, habit, clothing, and mien, without even the clarifying grace of being foreign. This sizable segment of the Negro population is probably shut out of the effective job market not so much because of the lack of specific work skills as because of the lack of specific social skills. This is the same segment of the Negro population which is a square peg in the round hole of the American school system because of characteristics resulting from Black Isolation, compounded by Black Pessimism.

These unique black community attributes are not irreversible, any more than are the attributes of the white community or its economy. The stability of the intellectual and cultural isolation of the Negroes has broken down at a number of points. The surveys indicate that at least three quarters of the Negro population, while wary, expect to make substantial gains in the coming years, and they count those gains in terms of entering the main American system. And the Black Anger, except as evidenced in the ideology of a few, still hangs on that eventuality.

The indications are that the Negro population is beginning to emerge and move into American society in the traditional pattern of past immigrant groups. If this generation in the ghettoes can be called, shamefully, a first generation—perhaps on the grounds that it has now substantially transformed itself from the dimensions of a caste to the dimensions of a submerged and emerging ethnic group—then second- and third-generation advances resembling those made by earlier Irish and Italian groups, for example, can be made. The signals are in the upward mobility indices: rising rates of educational achievement, of occupational advancement, of home ownership.

There are several heavily qualifying points that have to be made about this prognostication. First, there may not be time for second- and third-generation advances similar to those of earlier immigrant groups. Black Anger (like "black nationalism") is still a fragmented phenomenon. Specifically, there is *the* Black Anger of the educated or sophisticated young ideologues who are essentially radical, with a more or less black twist, in their approach to the total American system. This shades off into the ghetto anger of the less educated and less sophisticated young men on the streets, many of whom may be backing into the ideology after finding that their anger is more potent when it is Black. They are the spearpoint of the larger, older ghetto population whose frustrations can turn at any given point to anger, if the divisions are made sharp enough, to Black Anger. This population is the revolutionary's dream. In the 1930s, the revolutionaries failed because they couldn't engender a discrete enough lower class polarization, partly because of their own internal ambiguities. The black radicals have no such ambiguities (unlike the middle-aged and middle-class Negroes and whites who echo Black Anger)—and they see the necessary polarization at hand. Stokely Carmichael sees the polarization depending on a chain of white action and Negro reaction. He speaks openly of his hope of goading the whites into the kind of police action that will mobilize a more cohesive Black Anger.

There is another aspect of black attributes that denies the applicability of the traditional pattern of immigrant advancement. Partly because of the deep cultural isolation, there prevails among the critical mass of angry young Negroes—those who are not ideological and not upwardly mobile—an exaggerated sense of white happiness. There is a strong tendency to believe that white lower middle-class life is easier, more glamorous, and more affluent than it is. This in part accounts for the frequent dissatisfaction with entering the system at what seem to be low and grubby rungs. But coupled with that is the staple of Black Anger: if the American society did it to us deliberately, and admits having it done to us, then reparations are due, and now, not opportunity but reparations. Such reparations don't call for some "natural process" of advancement, but for a compensatory "leap forward" of a kind that has never taken place in the American society.

In the reparations demand, it has been noted that, while absolute statistical progress has been made by the Negro community in occupational status, education, and so forth, there has not been enough *relative* progress with respect to the whites who have also been progressing. It is likely, however, that second- and third-generation Irish and Italian immigrants never "caught up" with the native white population of the cities. They probably still haven't caught up economically, occupationally, educationally. As groups, they became a stable part of the system, in some relatively lower pattern, and progressed as the entire system progressed, making *relative* advancement as more and more individuals "trickled upward" in the system. That road to equality is a multigenerational one, but it's the only one that America or any society had ever offered to new, formerly depressed, population groups.

In short, there are indications that the Negro population is now on that road, that an appreciable number of Negroes are moving stably into the system, and that the individual trickle upward has begun. But there are also indications that there is not enough time for the traditional process to take place. The Negro stance is understandably not the stance of the old immigrant groups. The bulk of the Negro population, especially the youth, are not enchanted by historical prospects or sociological processes. There is a war on for the Negro mind. No one can be sure what would happen if black radicalism won that war, or at least acquired enough strength to wage it seriously. The chances are that, joined with extremist white backlash and the state of the world, the consequences would be considered disastrous by all reasonable men.

But for whatever reason, the fact remains that there is great urgency in many quarters to engineer a drastic hastening of the integration of Negroes into American society. There has been an outpouring of programs and an even greater outpouring of proposals for programs. A couple of billion dollars have been invested.

These questions then deserve to be raised: *Is* there any way in which a depressed population group can be propelled by an automated leap forward into the center of the system? Even if the two billion were fifty billion? Is there any way to accelerate the current Negro trickle upward into the system? Are the couple of billions being spent most profitably toward that end? Can we—and by what means—hold the society together while that process is going on? Why do so many of our current programs seem to be failing?

"The System" and the Cinderella Myth

If there is a single key to these questions, it lies in the nature of "the system" which is under such constant reference.

The system has two prime characteristics. In the first place, it describes the web of correlations, of dense mutuality, that exists among the agenda items called "urban problems": Income-education-occupation-housing-welfare-crime-health-family-tone-participation-status. For any given group this is a constellation of interacting factors, but the complex nature of the interaction is crucial. It is often taken for granted that if one can engineer changes in one accessible part of this system, it will affect the other parts. Thus, if educational achievement is advanced, then occupational status will be advanced, and so forth. If housing is improved, or health, then all other conditions will respond.

But the formula simply doesn't work. It certainly doesn't work well enough to solve any speedup problems. The research indicates that the significant causal factors related to group educational advancement are those considered the *end* products of education: the occupation and the educational traditions of the family. A few groups came to America already equipped with such traditions, notably the Jews and the Chinese. Others didn't. Their group educational status tended to rise *after* their group occupational status rose.

Of course, if educational achievement could be accelerated spectacularly, it undoubtedly would affect occupational and other patterns. The fallacy seems to lie in the belief that single elements can be torn out of the system and massively altered by direct remedy. This is the Social Engineering Fallacy, the Cinderella myth as rendered by social reformers. In the current era, for example, the indications are that direct educational remedies, whether better school plants, or smaller classes, or more funds, don't help all that much. The other unadjusted elements of the system that bear on education are too powerful.

Housing provides another kind of example. The assumption is often made that better housing means less delinquency, better health, and so forth. The evidence does not point to this result. If the same families in the same situation live in better housing, they produce substantially no less delinquency and enjoy no better health. But, more than that, better housing typically becomes deteriorated housing when the other life conditions of the tenants do not change.

Occupation is obviously the operational key to this system, and even it is not exempt from the Social Engineering Fallacy.

For example, day after day around the country, jobs are offered unskilled young people who want jobs but don't take them, or who take them and then drop out.

Of course, the system does spiral upward. It has for all the other emerging groups, and it is even doing so for the Negro. But the spiral has always seemed to be "spontaneous," the result of some "natural" social process.

Obviously, the appearance of spontaneity is somewhat exaggerated. Social planning and government intervention have played a significant role in the system's spiral at various times. The creation of a free secondary and higher educational system is an example. But typically these interventions have worked slowly and indirectly in effecting any group metamorphosis, by meshing in with, rather than disrupting, the natural rhythm and dense mutuality of the system. The provision of a free secondary educational system did not directly advance academic achievement as much as it accommodated favorably and progressively to the spiral already in existence. The expansion of free education was at once the result of the preceding entry of new groups into economic prominence and an opportunity for them to further extend that entry.

The nature of the Social Engineering Fallacy is twofold. In the first instance it supposes that an improved school system will in itself improve educational achievement, improved opportunity will improve occupational status, and so forth. This formula simply overlooks the highly correlative system embracing the total life of any population group. But there can also be the slightly more sophisticated supposition that if program assaults are made simultaneously on all accessible fronts, such as employment, housing, and education, *then* the system will automatically move apace for any group. The flaw here is that not all of the elements of mutuality in this correlative system are "objective" conditions. For example, family style, traditions, and group culture are, by nature, matters of generational transmission, respond sluggishly to changes, and are best approached by flanking rather than by direct attack.

The Social Engineering Fallacy can be stated modestly: If not as an iron law, then as a strong tendency, and admonition of moderation. The current instinct in America has been, to the contrary, that the application of more money, more programs, more services will solve each given problem. There isn't that kind of relationship between health and medical services, housing and housing services, education and educational services, or employment and employment services. These services become commodities that people desire as good in themselves, and that desire has its own legitimacy; but when a submerged group also depends on such services to produce drastic and specific results, most often what ensues is a Cinderella's coach effect—glittering promise, and then, a pumpkin.

The regular process of group advancement will take time, and if there is no irregular process that seems to work or work fast, are we then hopelessly lost? Only if we take literally the instant reparation demands emanating from the Negro community; or if we sit back and decide to let nature take its course, ignoring the symbolic and expressive aspects of those demands.

The American System

At this point it would be pertinent to extend the definition of "the system." It has already been seen as a highly correlative system, wherein group habits and styles change slowly in response to each other and to changing objective conditions, and wherein the change in objective conditions is heavily constrained by group habits and styles. Everybody is in such a correlative system of one kind or another; but not everybody is in *the* American system, which describes, in addition, a set of particular benevolent conditions existing partly in the mind, partly as a social reality. *The* American system is the main system, the spiral-upward system, and the pertinent question is whether a given population group is *in* that system at even a beginning stage, or whether it is outside in some frozen subsystem, as the Negro population has been for so long.

A chief characteristic of the perceived American system is that it is egalitarian in opportunity and upwardly mobile in fact. New population groups can enter it, prepare themselves for competition, and presumably move wherever their patterns of capability and aspirations will naturally take them. But, in fact, it has always been the mobility in itself, rather than any absolute state of economic equality, that has been critical. It has been the fact of entry and of movement, rather than of actual distribution at any point, that has always determined a population group's sense of being *in* the system. The criterion has been the apparent openness of the system, as symbolized by improving group stability in employment and economic status and an increasing number of individuals trickling upward.

As a statistical group, the Negro population is now beginning to take part in this process; but there is a difference created by their unique historical attributes. Because they have been excluded from the system for so long, the credibility gap for the Negro population is still immense. No other ethnic group was ever, or ever had to be, so organized for intrusion into the system; therefore, no other ethnic group was ever so literally and fervidly American in its ideological reading of the system. The demand for quota distribution throughout the economic system is unique to the Negro. Unique also is the depth of the division between those in the Negro community who are trickling up and those who still see themselves caught in a frozen subsystem. Relative position, rather than movement, was never so important a criterion for being *in* the system. But the quota demands are clearly hyperbole, and the overwhelming aspiration of the Negro population is still entry rather than some absolute position of economic equality. The special necessity then—and the only possibility—is to take actions that will convince the Negro population that it is indeed now, finally, in the system, even if it is not yet going to share equally in that system.

Pertinent to that effort is the fact that there is another major characteristic of *the* American system. *The* American system is seen as a system of individual effort, individual achievement, and self-dependency. The concept of mobility is still built around this image. However managed or cozened, self-dependency is still understood as the only way of establishing oneself as an integral part of the society. Through the protective haze of medicare, social security, unemployment insurance, and subsidized universities, the spirit of Horatio Alger is still perceived as *the* American spirit. A man must somehow make it on his own, or he hasn't made it.

This might change, of course. And there are those who say that it should change because it hasn't worked. But for the most part, they don't mean that. Some mean that the American system hasn't worked for the Negro, which it hasn't, but the Negro is just being let in. Others, the more affluent young critics, are really complaining that the system is too successful and has washed out more important human values. That may well be true—although one would first like to see the shape of some suggested substitute system and evaluate its implications for human values—but it's also irrelevant to the problem at hand. This *is* the American system, and *this* is the system that Negroes want to enter. In this perception as well, the Negro population is extremely American. When they say, "We don't want a handout," they mean it. Getting a handout means that you're not part of the system, you're still tacked on to some dependent subsystem. Still deep in the cotton fields.

The Program Implications

Programs will therefore tend to work, to help convince the Negro population that it's *in,* to the extent that the programs are geared toward, rather than away from, *the* American system. For example, neither more public housing nor rent supplement programs are, in that sense, systemic. People own their own homes in proper America. Individual home ownership payments are presumably preferable; a pattern of income that will sustain a self-dependent pattern of housing is even more preferable. This tends toward the kind of stake in society that serves to make a house a home. And, finally, it is not sheer money at all, but that symbolic stake in the society, as measured by some normative position in the perceived American system, that is all-important. It is a saving grace of the human quality that this is so; but it is also a practical point. Increased welfare payments, while necessary and humanitarian in lieu of anything else, are antisystemic and won't work for purposes of group advancement. In those cities where welfare families receive funds somewhat above the official poverty line, the situation seems no more rehabilitating than where families receive substantially lower welfare payments. Income maintenance plans, while more civilized and simply more efficient, are no more systemic.

It might seem easiest to create a stake by providing a job, but that has wide systemic variations too. Make-work job programs are obviously not systemic, and for the Negro population, now more Doubting Thomas than Uncle Tom, neither are various manpower training programs that are not sufficiently job connected. For the critical mass of young Negro people who want to become part of the system, but who don't have the appropriate cultural attributes, only systemic jobs will do, jobs that are related to special programs of on-the-job training and supervision. And private industry, buttressed by whatever governmental incentives, can do this total job more systemically than can government welfare agencies. And if government is going to take up the slack, it will do it more effectively in this era not with a WPA, but with a PWA of a more extended and permanent stature than that of the 1930s.

"Participation" has been emerging as an intended means of increasing the Negro population's sense of being included in, but this device has its special systemic variations, too, and some special problems. *The* American system, in all of its parts, is an integrated system—or else you're not in it at all. To develop separate ethnic power within the integrated American system, as did the Catholics, the Italians, and the Jews, is one thing. To try to develop a separate Black System is antisystemic on its face. Some programs have an ideological overlay that promotes this self-defeating direction. But there is obviously opportunity for extending the simple concept of more participation to many programs which would give them a symbolic importance outstripping their substantive effect.

None of these programs, however, with or without participation, and even of Marshall Plan proportions, is going to turn a multigenerational problem into one that can be solved in anybody's four-year administration. That's truth number one and a difficult one. Understanding that truth has the limited but still considerable importance that understanding any negative truth has. The system, as it is now working, if it keeps working, will undoubtedly do more to bring the Negro fully into the society in the long run than all the special programs we can invent.

But we will still continue to invent special programs, and for good reasons. First of all, there is the simple compulsion of activity in the face of seeming disaster. The society has the need to "do something." The Negro community has the need for "things to be done." And in the latter case especially, this activity *can* be profitable in its own limited way. Long-range and progressive adjustments in our system can ensue. For example, our schools can become more flexible to individual needs, or more oriented toward becoming full-time neighborhood community institutions as a result of some of these programs. Some of the programs, with respect to on-the-job training, for example, or special encouragement and assistance for college attendance, can actually accelerate the trickle upward for a given number of young people. But, most important, these programs can help bridge the inevitable time gap by providing some solid symbolic evidence to the Negro community that they are *in* and on the move. If that's not enough, then we *are* in trouble; it's in the nature of the problem that we can do no more than that. The current reading of the Negro community is that it *would* be enough, if we can handle the sporadic intervening problems of public order with wisdom. But the analysis strongly suggests that these special programs toward that end be devised more consciously with that end in mind, and less with panic and general program-mania. Without being oriented toward the systemic, these programs in their sum can have no effect at all, or a counter effect. It would at least seem worthwhile for the planners and policy makers, not to mention the social action groups, to understand more clearly where they're headed and why, what the priorities are, and the meaning of the alternatives. If our energies are spent too much in spinning myths and creating Cinderella's coaches, we may be exacerbating the problem we're attempting to treat.

Minority Group Psychology: Implications for Social Action

Alvin F. Poussaint, M.D.

Tufts University

Much has been written about the black man's psychic reactions to being a member of an oppressed minority in a white man's land.[1] The position of the Negro is unique among minority groups in America because he alone bears the scars of a slave heritage and wears the indelible mark of oppression, his black skin. It is impossible to discuss in this short paper all the aspects and implications of the Negro's psychological adaptation to white racism. Therefore, in view of the national crisis in race relations and the black rebellions taking place in our cities, I would like to focus on what I consider those key aspects of the psychology of black Americans having special relevance for the formulation of programmatic solutions to the urban crisis.

Historical Background

The system of slavery in its original form and as its remnants exist today had three dramatic consequences for the

[1] Work on this topic was originally commissioned by the Center for Policy Studies, University of Chicago. The author presented a paper with similar title at the Center's Conference on Short Term Measures to Avert Urban Violence in November, 1967.

black man's psyche. It generated in him (1) self-hatred and negative self-esteem, (2) suppressed aggression and rage, and (3) dependency and nonassertiveness. Although these manifestations are analytically distinguishable, they are, of course, not discrete phenomena, being interdependent and interrelated on many different levels. Thus, while we will deal with each in turn, a consideration of one necessarily involves reference to the others. (It should be understood that we are here dealing in generalities and that any individual could of course respond differently from what we see as predominant trends.)

Let us briefly look at the genesis and initial consequences of racism and examine Negroes' responses to it.

The castration of Afro-Americans and the resulting problems of negative self-image, suppressed aggression, and dependency started more than 350 years ago when black men, women, and children were wrenched from their native Africa, stripped bare both physically and psychologically, and placed in an alien white land. They thus came to occupy the most degraded of human conditions, that of a slave—a piece of property, a nonperson. Families were broken: black men were emasculated and black women were systematically exploited sexually and otherwise vilely degraded. The plantation system implanted and fostered the growth of a helplessness and subserviency in the minds of Negroes that made them dependent upon the good will and paternalism of the white man.[2] The more acquiescent the slave was, the more he was rewarded within the plantation culture. This practice forced the suppression of felt retaliatory rage and aggression in black men and women. Those who bowed and scraped for the white boss and denied their aggressive feelings were promoted to "house nigger" and "good nigger." Thus, within this system, it became a virtue for the black man to be docile and nonassertive. "Uncle Toms" are exemplars of these conditioned virtues. In order to retain the most menial of jobs and keep from starving, black people quickly learned such servile responses as "Yassuh, Massa." Thus, from the days of slavery to the present, passivity (and the resultant dependency) became a necessary survival technique.

By 1863, when slavery was abolished, the Afro-American had been stripped of his culture and left an oppressed black man in

[2] The present welfare system is in many ways analogous to this system in that it perpetuates this psychological dependency.

a hostile white man's world. He had, furthermore, learned to repress his aggression, behave subserviently, and view himself as an inferior. These things had been inculcated under the duress of slavery. All of these teachings were, however, reinforced after "freedom" when Jim Crow was born in the late 1800s and early 1900s. In the days following Reconstruction the systematized racist and sometimes psychotic propaganda of the white man, haranguing about the inferiority of the Negro, increased in intensity. He was disenfranchised, terrorized, mutilated, and lynched. The black man became every unacceptable, pernicious idea and impulse that the white man's psyche wished to project, that is, the Negro was an animal, violent, murderous, with ravaging sexual impulses. The intensity of the white man's psychological need that the Negro be shaped in the image of this projected mental sickness was such as to inspire the whole Jim Crow system of organized discrimination, segregation, and exclusion of Negroes from society.

In the resulting color caste system, white supremacists constructed an entire "racial etiquette" constantly to remind Negroes that they are only castrated humans. In their daily lives, Negroes are called "girl" and "boy" by whites. In the South, in particular, they are addressed by their first name by whites no matter how lowly that white person is. Negroes in turn are, however, expected to use courtesy titles such as Mr., Mrs., or Miss when addressing whites. White racists through the centuries have perpetrated violence on those blacks who demonstrate aggressiveness or insubordination. To be an "uppity nigger" was considered by white supremacists one of the gravest violations of the racial etiquette. Negro mothers learned to instruct their two- and three-year-old children to "behave" and say " 'yes sir and no sir' when the white man talks to you." Similarly, various forms of religious worship in the Negro community have fostered passivity in blacks and encouraged them to look to an afterlife for eventual salvation and happiness. Negroes have even been taught that they must love their oppressor and that it is "sinful" to hate or show appropriate anger.

In addition to demanding nonaggression and subservience, whites also inculcated in the Negro self-hatred and low self-esteem. They made certain that any wares allotted to the Negro were inferior. The Caucasian American socialized the black man to internalize and believe the many deprecating things that were said about him. They encouraged and rewarded behavior and attitudes in Negroes that substantiated these indicting stereotypes. Thus black men were happy-go-lucky and were laughed at by whites. Negroes were lazy, stupid, and irresponsible, and whites bemoaned this, but "put up with it" in a good-natured "noblesse oblige" fashion. Our mass media vigorously reinforced these images with such characters as Amos and Andy, Stepin Fetchit, and Beulah. In this way many Negroes were conditioned to believe, "Yes, I am inferior."

Not only were black men taught that black was evil and that Negroes were "no-good," they were also continually brainwashed into believing that only "white is right." This psychological feat was accomplished by allowing light-skinned Negroes with straight hair to elevate themselves in society above darker Negroes. As this happened, the whites suggested, and Negroes came to believe, that such blacks were better because they had much white blood. Thus, for the darker Negroes, their lack of social and economic success and their deprived conditions came to be associated with their Negroid qualities. Consequently Negroes exhibited profound shame in the vestiges of their African identity and sought to hide or deny these. Without the positive history of their former African culture and its achievements to raise their self-esteem, and with the achievements of both the white men and the "whiter Negroes" staring them in the face, black men sought to be white. They revered Caucasian characteristics—pale skins, straight hair, aquiline features—and despised their own curly hair, broad noses, and full lips.

The most tragic, yet predictable, part of all of this structuring is that the Negro has come to form his self-image and self-concept on the basis of what white racists have prescribed; therefore, black men and women learn quickly to hate themselves and each other because they are black.

These, then, are the broad historical outlines of certain aspects of the black man's situation in the United States, those related to his socialization in an oppressive system and having consequences for his psychological development. We have briefly discussed those patterned and institutionalized stimuli present over the years in black-white interaction which gave rise in the Negro to such learned habits of response as self-hatred and negative self-esteem, suppressed rage, and subserviency. In the following sections some of the more critical dynamics and manifestations of these characteristics are discussed, with special emphasis on those having implications for social action planning.

Negro Self-Image

Although the Negro's self-concept is affected by factors associated with poverty and low economic class status, blackness in itself has consequences for ego development not inherent in lower class membership. The black person develops in a color caste system and usually acquires the negative self-esteem that is the natural outcome of membership in the lowest stratum of such a system. Through contact with such institutionalized symbols of caste inferiority as segregated schools, neighborhoods, and jobs and more indirect negative indicators such as the reactions of his own family, he gradually becomes aware of the social and psychological implications of his racial membership. He is likely to see himself as an object of scorn and disparagement, unwelcome in a white high caste society and unworthy of love and affection. The young Negro child learns very early in life to despise himself and to reject those like himself. From that time on, his entire personality and style of interaction with his environment became molded and shaped in a warped, self-hating, and self-denigrating way.

Sometimes this self-hatred can take on very subtle manifestations. For instance, competition, which may bring success, may also bring failure. Thus the efforts that may bring success to a black man are often not made even when the opportunity exists. There are, no doubt, two reasons for this failure to act: First, the anxiety that accompanies growth and change is avoided if a new failure is not risked; therefore, a try is not made. Second, the steady state of failure represented by nonachievement (and defined by someone other than yourself) rather than by an unsuccessful trial, is what many Negroes have come to know and expect, and so they feel safer (less psychologically discomforted) with the more familiar. Furthermore it has often meant survival to black men to deny the possession of brains, thoughts, and feelings, thus making it difficult to move from a position of passivity to one of activity and to acknowledge heretofore forbidden feelings and behavior as now safe, legitimate, and acceptable.

It is all too frequent that Negroes with ability, intelligence, and talent do not aspire to the full extent of their potential. Being unused to occupying positions of prestige and responsibility, many Afro-Americans have lower aspirations than their talents and abilities warrant. They tend to shy away from competition, particularly with white people, and often feel insecure even when their abilities and success have been acknowledged. In fact, at least one study has demonstrated that, even when Negroes are given objective evidence of their equal intellectual ability in an interracial situation, they typically continue to feel inadequate and to react submissively.[3] This lack of aggressiveness may also account at least in part for Negroes' below par achievement in school. Negro girls, however, who are not as threatening to whites and therefore not as systematically crushed as Negro boys, have been found to exceed Negro boys in achievement at all grade levels through college.[4] Thus their low aspirations and achievement may be attributable not only to their own feelings of inferiority, but also to a learned inability to be normally aggressive. Many psychiatrists feel that self-denigration in Negroes is associated primarily with the more general castration of the black man by white society. Some even believe that the self-hatred should be viewed as *rage* turned inward, rather than as primarily their shame in being black and their desire to be white. Let us look further at this relationship of rage to self-hatred.

Self-Hatred and Rage

Even if a Negro does not start out with self-hatred feelings, these can develop from compromising with a suppressive society. A Negro with all the self-love and self-confidence in the world cannot express legitimate feelings of anger or rage in a system that is brutally and unstintingly suppressive of self-as-

[3] I. Katz and L. Benjamin, "Effects of White Authoritarianism in Biracial Work Groups," *J. Abnormal and Soc. Psych.*, 61:448, 1960.

[4] T. F. Pettigrew, *A Profile of the Negro American* (Princeton: D. Van Nostrand Co., Inc., 1964).

sertion; therefore, after a while, even a confident Negro would have to hate himself for biting his tongue and not expressing himself in an appropriate way. Even though talking back to a white man, in the South for example, may mean his life and keeping quiet is the most sensible self-preservatory response, a person has to hate not only the person who forces him to be silent, but also *himself* for acquiescing and compromising his integrity. This is the self-hatred that comes from a feeling of helplessness and powerlessness in the face of overwhelming oppression. The whole system of southern legal justice has been designed—and still functions—to inflict severe and inequitable penalties on Negroes showing even minor aggression toward whites. Negroes who dare to show their anger at whites are usually punished out of proportion to their "crime." Even in the North, blacks who are "too outspoken" about racial injustices often lose their jobs or are not promoted to higher positions because they are considered "unreasonable" or "too sensitive." It is significant that the civil rights movement had to adopt passive resistance and nonviolence in order to win acceptance by white America. But, alas, even here, there was too much "aggression" shown by Negroes. Whites recoiled and accused civil rights groups of "provoking violence" by peaceful protest.

These responses are, of course, related to tendencies to be dependent and subservient. The inability of Negroes to be self-assertive has fostered a dependency which has had devastating consequences for the social behavior and psychic responses of Negroes. It has been found, for instance, that Negroes are less likely to go into business or entrepreneurial ventures.[5] This is the result, no doubt, of their trained incapacity to be assertive, assertiveness being essential to the entrepreneurial spirit. For example, a Negro may be afraid to make a decision without checking with a white man, or being assured of white approval.

The demands of being unwillingly subservient, unwillingly self-denigrating, and unwillingly nonaggressive are psychically extremely taxing. Frustration and anger are the obvious byproducts of the requirement to be less than a man, less than human. Thus we come to an obvious question: What does the black man do with his anger and aggression?

[5] N. Glazer and D. P. Moynihan, *Beyond the Melting Pot* (Cambridge: Massachusetts Institute of Technology Press, 1963).

Dealing with Anger and Aggression

The simplest method for dealing with rage is to suppress it and substitute an opposing emotional attitude—compliance, docility, or a "loving attitude." Sometimes anger can be denied completely and replaced by a compensatory happy-go-lucky disposition, flippancy or—an attitude extremely popular among Negroes—"being cool." Another way for aggression to be channeled is through competitive sports, music, or dancing. These are the few activities white society has traditionally opened to Negroes. Another acceptable means of channeling rage is to identify with the oppressor and put all of one's energy into striving to be like him. A third means for the oppressed to give expression to their feelings is to emphathize or identify with someone objectively like themselves (black), who for one reason or another is free to express appropriate rage directly at the oppressor. Malcolm X and Adam Clayton Powell served this function. Still another technique for dealing with anger is to replace it with a type of chronic resentment and stubbornness toward white people, interpreted as a "chip on the shoulder." Trying to control rage in this way frequently shows itself in a general irritability and always has the potential of becoming explosive. Thus, the spreading wave of riots in Negro ghettos may be seen as outbursts of suppressed rage. Although these riots are contained in the ghetto, the hatred is usually directed at those whom the rioters see as controlling and oppressing him economically, psychologically, and physically—store owners and policemen.

Sometimes suppressed emotions will be expressed in such psychosomatic symptoms as headaches, low back pain, and diarrhea. Rage is also directed inward in such deviations as alcoholism, drug addiction, and excessive gambling, and also in the tendency of Negroes to distrust and hate other blacks more than they do their white oppressors. In psychiatric practice it is a generally accepted principle that a chronic repressed rage will eventually lead to a low self-esteem, depression, emotional dullness, and apathy.

It appears now as if more and more Negroes are freeing themselves of suppressed rage through greater outspoken release of pent-up emotions. Perhaps this is an indication that self-love is beginning to outbalance self-hate in the black man's soul. The old passivity is fading and being replaced by a drive to undo centuries of powerlessness, helplessness, and dependency under American racism.

Approaches to the Problem

If we believe that self-hatred, suppressed rage, nonassertiveness, and dependency are at the core of many of the black man's social and psychological difficulties, what can American society do to remove some of these scars from the black psyche? What programs in the black community itself will foster a positive self-image, channel rage, and encourage constructive self-assertion? The answers to these questions are obviously not simple ones and perhaps they will require a serious examination of the basic value system of American society. But some answers are suggested by a consideration of the consequences of the two major philosophies underlying social action programs designed to change the position of the Negro in the United States. There are, first, those whose aims are integration of the black man into society, and second, those who aim to improve the position of the black man in society, but do not emphasize his integration into it. Let us first look at the integrationist orientation.

Integration and Assimilation

The civil rights gains in the past decade, and especially in the 1960s, have done much to modify the negative self-concepts of Afro-Americans. The civil rights movement itself has brought a new sense of dignity and respect to those blacks most severely deprived by poverty and oppression in the rural South and northern ghetto. One factor that may have been significant in improving the self-image of the masses of Negroes was that black men were leading this struggle, rather than white men. This fact in itself probably made Negroes, through the process of identification, take more pride in their group and feel less helpless, for they could see black men, through *their* efforts, knowing more and bringing about positive changes in their environment. The feeling of "fate control," that is, that one can have "control" over social forces rather than be a victim of them, is crucial to one's feelings of ego-strength and self-esteem. Thus, the movement brought to the Negro a new sense of power in a country dominated by a resistant white majority. The movement also acted to channel the expressions of assertiveness among Negroes even if this expression came mainly through nonviolent protest. Beyond these achievements, however, civil rights leaders at that time tended to see total integration of the black and white races as the final step in destroying the Negro's negative self-esteem and dependency on white authority.

Now we have seen emerge in segments of the civil rights movement a disenchantment with the social and psychological consequences of American "integration." This disenchantment arises, at least in part, from the fact that integration has moved at a snail's pace and has been marked by white resistance and tokenism. The Negro has found himself in the demeaning and uncomfortable position of asking and demanding that the white man let him into *his* schools, *his* restaurants, *his* theaters, even though he knows that the white man does not want him. In both the South and the North, many Afro-Americans have resented the indignity of constantly being in the position of begging for acceptance into the white man's institutions. Such a posture placed blacks in the same old dependent relationship to the white man as when he asked for and expected food and protection from the slave master. Negroes have become further demoralized upon seeing that the recent civil rights laws did not effectively change this pattern of relationships with whites. It immediately became apparent that integration, especially in schools, was not to be integration in a real sense at all, but merely token placement of Negro children, that is, "one-way integration." Negro parents in the South and North, for example, rarely speak of sending their children to the "integrated school": they say, "My child is going to the *white* school." In the overwhelming majority of instances, no white children are "integrated" into Negro schools. Since integration is only a one-way street that Negroes travel to a white institution, then inherent in the situation itself is the implied inferiority of the black man and the fact that *he* must seek out whites to better his position, the implication that only the Negro can benefit and learn, that he has nothing to offer whites and they have nothing to learn from him. Thus an already negative self-image is reinforced.

Parents who fear psychological harm to their children are not anxious to send them to "integrated" schools. Some of the college aged young people in the movement stated frankly that they find this type of integration personally degrading and do not want to go to any school where they have to be "accepted by white racists." It must be remembered that black people are seeking not only social and economic help but psychological salvation. The Negro is not only demanding equal rights but is desperately searching for *inner* emancipation and escape from the chronic effects of white racism upon his psyche. In this search for peace, many young blacks (even on our college campuses) feel a need to insulate themselves from the subtle expressions of racism they experience in their daily encounters with whites. In this context the growth of black organizations on campuses takes on a significance notably different from the one of "racist separatism" often imputed by the press. Perhaps this isolation serves to protect them from feelings of self-consciousness which they experience in the presence of whites. Such uncomfortable feelings prevent them from feeling relaxed and thus "being themselves."

Since the number of Negroes at any white school is token, particular hardships are created for these individuals. They immediately find themselves surrounded by children who are generally the products of white racist homes. In this situation, since all children want to belong, the Negro must become an expert at "being liked and accepted." In such a social setting, if the self-esteem of the black student grows, it is likely to be not so much from feelings of comfort and satisfaction in being Negro as it is from his own conditioned beliefs that "white is right" and that he has succeeded in a white world; thus he is either a successful pioneer or a martyr.

Those people who offer assimilation as a solution must examine what they are asking Negroes to do. Many Negroes, including segments of both the old civil rights movement and nationalists, are beginning to fear that "token integration" may augment the identity problems of the Negro. Such integration as has existed in the North has not substantially helped to solve the Negro's identity problems. Assimilation by definition takes place into and according to the larger societal (white) model of culture and behavior. Thus, if Negroes are to assimilate, it is they who must give up their black identity and subculture to be comfortably integrated. Many Negroes who seek complete assimilation thus become preoccupied with proving to white people that they are just like all other human beings, that is, white, and worthy of being assimilated. At the same time they express their willingness to give up all elements of their black identity. This in itself means to them that they are giving up something of inferior or negative value to gain something of greater value: a white identity.

In seeking acceptance among whites, many Afro-Americans expend a great deal of internal energy trying to prove that they are all right; but this effort is vain and fruitless because personal acceptability must be repeatedly proven to each new group of whites. Thus, before a Negro can be an individual he must first prove that he is a human. The Negro groups' vigorous pursuit of middle-class status symbols is frequently an overdetermined attempt to demonstrate to the white man, as well as to themselves, that they can be successful, worthwhile human beings. White America, however, has lumped all Negroes together into one collective group. Hence, there can be no individual freedom for any one Negro until there is group freedom for all.

That an individual can achieve individual status only through changing his group's status, is, however, an idea foreign to American thought. The Negro, like other Americans, has accepted the belief (descended from the tenets of the Protestant ethic) that individuals succeed or fail solely as a result of their individual efforts. Thus, an individual's worth is assessed solely on the basis of his merits: he is accepted or rejected because of what he is as an individual. The acceptance by the Negro of this idea of individual merit has worked to his detriment, for it has operated to sustain a delusion in the face of a contradicting reality. It would perhaps be more realistic for black people to develop and orient themselves in terms of overcoming barriers to them as a group. Only then will acceptance or rejection as *individuals* follow. Achievement of this group freedom, however, requires undoing racial self-hatred, expending greater group assertiveness for social and political action, and adopting a positive and proud stance toward themselves and others.

Those individuals and organizations who reject the integration philosophy for improving the position of Negroes in American society focus on the achievement of group freedom, maintaining that only through strength as a group can black men win human dignity and power. Among these advocates would be those who are committed to the philosophy of "black power" or "black consciousness."

Black Consciousness or Black Power

As we mentioned, an important issue in the emancipation of black people is self-determination and fate control. Black consciousness movement supporters argue that as long as Negroes are powerless politically and do not have a degree of control over their own communities, they will remain psychological beggars in a white man's house. For instance, they ask, why shouldn't the black community have the final word about the type of policemen that are permitted in their community? Why should a white man downtown be able to send white racist police who shout or think "nigger" into the black community to "enforce the law?" Why, they reason, can't black communities have some degree of autonomy in governing their community, particularly since white-controlled urban governments have vested interests in protecting the majority white interests? Who is watching out for black interests? Following the same line of reasoning, black consciousness supporters maintain that local groups should have some say in deciding who will teach in their schools, who will run local welfare departments, in short, who will control their local institutions. To many blacks this does not represent "separatism"; it is simply democracy. The next question, however, is whether or not all-black institutions can provide Negroes with a more stable, positive sense of identity and self-esteem.

It is known that such groups and individuals as the Black Muslims and Malcolm X have frequently had many positive and constructive effects on members of the black community. This group has brought greater self-reliance and dignity to hard-core, untouchable segments of the Negro community. The Muslims were once the one major Negro group (now there are others of the black power orientation) that called for separation of the races and black self-sufficiency as an alternative approach to the remedy of the black man's problems of negative identity and self-esteem. Observers generally agree that the Muslims were quite effective in rehabilitating many antisocial and criminal types by fostering in them a positive self-image and pride in their blackness. This group also afforded blacks a channel for expressing their rage at the "white devils." The significant fact is that the Muslims were able to alleviate much of the individual Negro's self-hatred without holding up or espousing integration or "full acceptance" of the black man into American white society.

Other black consciousness groups have instilled pride and esteem in Negroes by emphasizing Negro history and achievements. Programs based on this philosophy can build Negro self-confidence and self-assertion by calling upon black men to think and do for themselves. They may also provide the stimulus for more independent thought and grass-roots problem-solving and lead to the development of community leadership. Such programs seem to have the potential for undoing much of the black man's self-hatred and emasculation, and these are the feelings that, in part, lead to behavior destructive of self and others. Finally, such "race consciousness" programs can constructively channel the Negro frustrations and anger that now lead to destructive violence and riots.

The question must be raised, however, whether all-black programs will in some ways lead to more identity and self-esteem problems for the Negro since such groups would always exist within a surrounding dominant white culture and would run the risk of being considered inferior. Can you really build a sense of community and pride in the ghettos when these neighborhoods carry the stigma of forced segregation by and from the white community? Can people develop a pride in a neighborhood made up of dilapidated housing usually in the most dismal part of our cities? Definitive answers to these questions cannot yet be given. We would suggest, however, that if Negroes were truly *equals* in the larger society, a black subculture could exist much in the same way that America has subcultures of other national and racial groups such as the Jews, Irish, Chinese, and so on. That is, if community derives from choice and is among people who feel common bonds, it can be a more salutary situation for blacks than if people of disparate interests, abilities, and needs are forced together in a ghetto solely on the basis of a common skin color.

News dispatches make it clear that, despite the drive for

racial integration, it is being vigorously resisted by the white population, particularly in the area of housing; therefore, we can expect to have isolated, predominantly black communities for a long time to come. Black power advocates hold that the potentiality of these communities cannot be ignored while integration is awaited. They insist on building strong black based institutions now. Whether these can become positive communities founded on common interests and supported by pride—or will remain run-down ghettos that are encampments of human misery—remains to be seen. But the answer rests with both black and whites: whether blacks will support this development, and whether whites will allow the movement to proceed without insuperable harassment.

Implications for Social Change

We have discussed in the preceding pages the psychological predispositions that have been generated in the Negro by virtue of his position and relationship in the American social system. We have also given some attention to the consequences of these psychic orientations and the programs and philosophies that have arisen to attempt to change them. It remains for us to suggest what we see as the implications of all this.

Since the black man's need for a sense of self-worth, self-assertion, and independence cannot be met through token integration and since assimilation appears to be a remote possibility, it seems logical that both black and white men must turn to the development and rehabilitation of Negro communities. In this endeavor, however, it is crucial that as much responsibility as possible be placed in the hands of black men, since self-development and self-determination lead to a greater sense of self-worth and power.

The white establishment can help to alleviate those problems that afflict black Americans by undoing white supremacy and the oppression of colored peoples. In doing so, white people will have to give up some share of their control and power over black communities. At the same time the white community must earnestly struggle for open housing so that Negroes can have a *free choice* about where they will live. With a choice, the many Negroes who choose to live among blacks will know that they have exercised their free will rather than that they have acquiesced to powers forcing them into a box.

In our cities, white officials can help to build the status of black communities by making them centers of business and cultural attraction for *all* the people. Why not have major theaters, museums, and trade centers located in black communities as part of a general rehabilitation program for the ghettos? There are many other small ways in which the black ghettos could be made part of the mainstream of our urban centers. Even though much has been said in the past decades about the urgent need for jobs, decent housing, and quality education and training programs, very little has been done to implement these ideas. The society is now paying with urban disorder and riots for this chronic neglect in alleviating some of these basic problems.

The availability of jobs is especially crucial for the black man in his struggle for dignity. Not only do jobs give men a sense of importance and self-worth, but they may also be a channel for the appropriate release of aggression. As in sublimation and displacement they may allow black men to express the assertiveness that has been so long dammed up. It is also obvious that if we are to do something to stabilize the Negro family we must begin by providing secure jobs for the black man. Men without work cannot fulfill their role and responsibility as husbands and fathers. The entire welfare system must be remodeled so that it will encourage the growth and independence of its recipients. These are only a few of the many social and economic programs that can be developed to alleviate these deplorable human conditions.

It becomes obvious after this long discussion of the psychology of a minority group that this subject cuts across broad social, economic, and political areas. The subject and its implications for social change cannot be considered in isolation. In order to relieve the psychic problems of Negroes that now manifest themselves in self-hatred, suppressed aggression, nonassertiveness, and dependence, we must address ourselves to the many ramifications of white racism in America.

The President's Commission on Civil Disorders has already made important recommendations for taking a decisive step in solving some of these problems; however, this arduous task requires the creative minds, brave spirits, and imaginative plans of all Americans who are sincerely concerned with the future of this country.

Municipal Objectives and Organization

The Functions of the City

Robert Dorfman

Harvard University

I take it for granted that something is wrong with the American city. Though we are in the midst of a war, the newspapers and magazines are devoting unaccustomed space to urban problems: safety in the streets, education, traffic congestion, air pollution, water supply, slums, and even the technical complications of urban finance. As is only natural, we are attempting to grapple with each of these problems on its own merits. Such an approach is appropriate because the means for dealing with, for example, air pollution and the inadequacies of the schools are disconnected, at least on a superficial level. But it is also inappropriate because the problems are clearly interconnected at a deeper level and because a piecemeal series of attacks is not a strategy and does not provide an intelligent order of priorities. It is in order, therefore, to search for the unifying elements in all these problems.

There is obviously one urban problem that dominates all the others in urgency and in importance: the predicament of the colored minority. This is clearly the source of the troubles in the streets, the decay of the central cities, the deterioration of the schools, and much else. Thus, any significant discussion of our cities must be focused on our race problem. But the race problem is not a peculiar property of the Negroes. The Puerto Ricans in Harlem and the Mexicans in California display many of the same social pathologies. It follows that we should look for the source of the problem not in the characteristics of the Negro but in those of the city, which is what I intend to do.

To this end we need a nonevaluative description of an American city, which will take the form of a highly simplified model to highlight the sources of the stresses we are experiencing.[1] These stresses result from the fact that a city performs a number of functions in our society whose demands are discordant with each other. Thus, we begin by inspecting the functions of a city.

A city can be regarded from four points of view. First, it is *a very elaborate physical, technological, and spatial layout.* From this aspect a city is a complex of buildings, wires, pipes, wireless communications, ventilation facilities, surface and subsurface means of access, and so on. It is a large and complicated machine for housing, maintaining, and transporting its population and for storing and transporting the materials they use and disposing of their wastes. In contrast with most other machines, a city comes into being by growth rather than by design and construction. As a result the parts are not well designed to fit each other; they are in varied states of disrepair and obsolescence, and they are replaced and modernized seriatim. Blighted areas and slums are a normal characteristic of a city just as obsolete components are a normal part of a large factory. In short, the physical aspect of a city is that of a great machine in a perpetual state of construction and chronic inadequacy; but, as Parkinson observed long before me, physical inadequacy is a sign of growth and vitality.

From a second point of view a city can be regarded as *a governmental or political entity.* From this point of view an American city is a fantastically complicated and unwieldy institution, a circumstance from which many of its difficulties flow. A survey of Cook County disclosed that there are more than 1,300 governmental jurisdictions, legally independent of each other, each of which discharges some governmental functions within the county. This situation is typical: our overlay of state, federal, municipal, county, sewage district, school district, and other jurisdictions guarantees it. Coordination among all these units is, of course, impossible. In fact, coordi-

[1] By "city" I shall always mean a standard metropolitan statistical area (SMSA) as used by the Census Bureau.

nation within any one of them, say the municipal government itself, is difficult because many of the officials are independently elected and have independent constituencies and authorities that render them only partially subject to the control of the mayor or other titular head. In short, governmentally, as well as physically, a city is a jumble of poorly integrated parts.

The foregoing two aspects of the city are, however, subsidiary and instrumental. The city as physical facilities and as governmental organization exists to serve the city's other two aspects: the city as *an economic unit* and the city as *a social unit.* It is to these two aspects, and particularly the second, that we have to pay the most attention. I shall argue that much of the complexity of city life results from the conflicting demands made upon the city by its economic and social functions.

The primary economic function of the city is to house one or more markets. A city is not a good place for a farm or a mine or even a factory. But for those economic activities that depend upon numerous contacts and flows of information, location in the right city is practically indispensable. In spite of all the marvels of electronics, it remains true that the everyday conduct of business requires quick, cheap, informal, and intimate communication between a business firm and its suppliers, customers, and even rivals. This kind of communication is going on all the time in the city, in its employment offices, its businessmen's restaurants, its display rooms, its stores, its streets, its conference rooms. Telephones and jet travel are all very well; but frequently in large affairs, and almost always in the multitude of small ones, it pays to be on the spot. Economists refer to the advantages of close contact as "economies of agglomeration." If you want to cast a TV serial, you had better be in Hollywood, where the actors are; and if you are an actor, you had better be there also because that is where the producers expect to find you. If you want buyers to see your dresses, you had better have a New York showroom. And so on.

Economically speaking, each city is a center or market of one sort or another, and the particular industries it serves define its primary economic functions. Or, in slightly different words, each city specializes in providing quick, cheap, day-to-day communication facilities for the firms in one or a few of the nation's economic sectors.

The economic function of the city is, therefore, to serve as the communication center, or market, for some industries. The size and character of the city are dictated to a large extent by the size and physical requirements of the markets it houses. Not only must it provide working space and communications for its industries, but it must provide living space, public utilities, protective services, and logistic support of every sort for the industries and for the people who staff them.

From the economic point of view the city is a marketplace and its population is the staff of the market and of the firms that participate in it. The inhabitants of the city are, therefore, in close day-to-day contact with each other in the course of performing their economic functions, and these contacts disregard, very largely, the social likes and dislikes of the people involved. These social likes and dislikes are, however, the essence of the fourth aspect of the city, its aspect when regarded as a social entity.

The most superficial glance at an American city will disclose that it includes a wide variety of people who sort themselves out into neighborhoods largely on the basis of ethnic affinity and socioeconomic similarity. These neighborhoods have neither economic nor administrative nor legal significance. They are social entities purely, and they discharge most of the social functions of the city insofar as they are discharged at all.

This clustering on grounds of ethnic and income similarity is the contemporary expression of one of mankind's most deep-seated urges: the need to be a loyal member of a well-defined and somewhat exclusive social group. I mention below some of the specific psychological satisfactions derived from such membership, but the central fact, which probably requires no further analysis, is that a man needs to attach himself emotionally to some tribe, clan, or community, and feels lost, isolated, and meaningless when he cannot do so. Once upon a time, I suppose, this trait had important survival value, for the ability of the clan to prey upon its competitors and resist their depredations depended upon the loyalty of its members. Nowadays the antagonistic aspect of group identification is disfunctional, though it persists and accounts for many of the characteristics of the American city. The constructive, communal-minded aspect remains essential.

The need for identification with a group accounts for the subdivision of the city into homogeneous neighborhoods. A group is a group of allies. It cannot be all-inclusive, for the vitality and solidarity of the alliance depend on the existence of potential enemies. As James Stephens once said, there cannot be an inside without an outside. Moreover, this same need explains why the neighborhoods must stand in very complicated relationships to one another. Overt and unmitigated enmity cannot be tolerated, but some amount of distrust, hostility, and xenophobia is part of the cement that solidifies the group.

The group or neighborhood provides other satisfactions to its members in addition to the general feeling of belonging to something and of purpose in life (namely, promoting the general welfare of the group). One of these is the comfort and security that comes from being among people who share rather than challenge our presuppositions, tastes, and values. This particular satisfaction dictates the formation of neighborhoods on the basis of similarity of ethnic and cultural backgrounds and also explains why virtually all of an individual's social life may be lived within the confines of his ethnic community.

In the second place, the group provides the anonymous individual with vicarious feelings of significance and accomplishment through his identification with talented or influential members of his group. And we should not overlook that the ethnic group provides a safe and socially accepted channel for expressing aggression. We all experience more frustrations and more occasions for rage than we can respond to under the conditions of modern urban life. Frustration cannot be bottled up indefinitely, but it can be displaced. When, for example, we should like to beat our wife or insult our boss, we can gain considerable relief from our necessarily suppressed rage by calumniating the members of some other social group. Under extreme provocation, we can even join a riot.

In short, there are real and important psychological needs —for identification, for approval and support, for discharge of hostility—that can be met by belonging to an appropriate social group. In a small and homogeneous town, the whole community may coalesce into such a group. In a large and diverse city, the populace divides itself into ethnically oriented neighborhoods (primarily) in its attempt to satisfy these needs. These neighborhoods are generally too amorphous and unstable, I should think, to provide much sense of communal effort or purpose. They do provide the security of being among people of similar beliefs and tastes, and they do provide outlets for deflected aggression, which are all the more important because of the feebleness of the positive, constructive satisfactions.

The functions mentioned so far all follow from perceiving a neighborhood or social group as one of a number of associated and competitive groups that occupy the same living space. There is another vital social function that any community must discharge, irrespective of the presence of competing groups: it must socialize its members, particularly its young. This is done by inculcating the traditions and culture of the community (including, importantly, loyalty to it) and by providing a sufficient variety of models of desirable behavior and of social roles so that an individual can find adequate scope for self-expression and personal development within the confines of his community. In our cities part of the task of social indoctrination is carried on by the city as a whole (for example, through its formal educational system) and part, less formally, by the ethnic neighborhoods which otherwise would atrophy. Models of personal development, however, have to be provided almost entirely by the ethnic communities because young people do not have sufficient contact with outsiders, nor can they, simply because they are outsiders, identify with them. It should be remarked at once that Negro communities are particularly deficient in models of social behavior and development.

From these considerations there emerges a simplified model of an American city. It consists of a cluster of ethnically distinguished neighborhoods whose members collaborate in staffing the firms, markets, and other economic and political organizations of the city. Economic cooperation brings the members of the diverse ethnic communities into intimate and daily contact with each other. Social predilections separate them at the end of the day. There emerges a delicate balancing of economic and social forces. On the one hand, the demands of economic life render the diverse groups dependent upon each other and enforce cooperation among them. On the other hand, competition for economic opportunity creates an arena for the virulent expression of social antagonism. The economic life of the city depends upon moderating the diverse tendencies, while social vitality reinforces them.

The tensions just described are mitigated, to an extent, by

carrying over into economic life the ethnic divisions of social life. Certain occupations and industries become segregated, just as neighborhoods are. It would be surprising if it were otherwise. People wish to work, as to live, among people with whom they feel most at ease. Some aspects of economic performance are transmitted in the cultures of the groups, as emphasis on scholarliness and bookishness among Jews. Wherever markets are imperfect, the tendency of members of any group to favor their fellows draws them together, just as the suspiciousness, prejudice, and competitiveness of members of each group against outsiders drives them apart. And, finally, just because personal contacts are much richer within groups than between them, the flows of information, which are an important part of markets and of city life, facilitate economic relationships within groups more than among them.

The consequence is that the diverse ethnic groups within the city come to dominate different industries and occupations. Though this fact has its regrettable side from the viewpoint of individualistic and egalitarian standards, it contributes to the viability of the city and to the stability and health of the social groups. It diminishes the tensions of the economic life of the city by reducing the frequency and intimacy of contacts between members of alien groups, that is, it extends to economic life some of the coziness of social life. But I attach more importance to its impact on the vitality of the ethnic groups which provide most of the social satisfactions of the city. The esteem and status of the group is derived in substantial part from its contribution to the economic life of its city, and in particular from the industries in which it plays a dominant role. Thus, the specialization of ethnic groups to industries is an important support to their self-regard and to their feelings of security and belongingness in the city as a whole. Furthermore, through this means the structure of economic status in the city as a whole is duplicated within its ethnic communities. The models of personal conduct and development that were mentioned above as one of the requisities for a healthy community are a by-product of this industrial specialization. They could be created without the specialization to be sure, and sometimes are; but their vividness and effectiveness are reinforced by the circumstance that the career pattern is part of the group culture and tradition, is contained largely within it, and includes some elements of exploitation of alien groups.

The economic and social functions of the city thus impinge very forcefully upon each other. The economic functions provide the city's unity and define the opportunities for the ethnic groups that comprise it. The social functions create the city's diversity and strongly influence all aspects of behavior, including economic.

This vision, or image, of the nature of the American city has implications for our understanding of what is wrong with it today and what can be done about it. In the first place it maintains that many of the important social functions of the city depend upon the vitality of the ethnic communities and neighborhoods within it. Integration, in the sense of cultural homogenization of the population, is not in the field of possibility in the visible future and may not even be desirable if, as this analysis suggests, a man needs to be a member of a psychologically manageable subgroup less diverse and overwhelming than an entire city.[2] It suggests, indeed, that the neighborhoods and subgroups in American cities are less vital and coherent than they should be if they are to provide their members with meaningful social satisfactions.[3] It suggests, furthermore, that since subgroups will persist so will tensions among them. If the social development of the cities can be influenced at all by conscious planning, which is doubtful, emphasis should be placed on strengthening the positive, constructive satisfactions of life within the ethnic neighborhoods so as to reduce the emotional importance of the hostility relations among them.

More specifically, it should be noted that the quality of housing has not come up in this discussion. Improvement of housing may well be desirable on various grounds, but this analysis implies that it is not one of the critical elements in our urban problem. Perhaps this is the reason public housing schemes have not had the beneficent social effects expected from them. Improvement of housing is an attractive social expedient because we know how to accomplish it simply by spending money; but it should not, for that reason, be made

[2] This conclusion is supported by the findings of Oscar Handlin, "The Goals of Integration," *Daedalus*, vol. 95 (winter, 1966), pp. 261–286, and Talcott Parsons, "True Citizenship for the Negro American? A Sociological Problem," *Daedalus*, vol. 94 (fall, 1965), pp. 1009–1054, in the *Daedalus* symposium on the Negro American.

[3] This finding is strictly in the tradition of Emile Durkheim.

the centerpiece of our attack on the problem of the cities if the problem actually lies elsewhere.

Formal education, also, has played only a small role in this analysis, which perhaps is fortunate because it is so terribly difficult to improve. The Coleman Report indicates that the success of formal education depends more on the cultural environment of the students than the other way round, which is a conclusion that this analysis tends to also. This, again, implies that the strategic focus of our attack should not be on the formal educational system.

Jobs are important as everyone knows, but this analysis indicates that not any old jobs will contribute to a lasting solution of our urban problems. Specifically, developing employment opportunities in the lowest occupational levels of scattered industries may contribute more to perpetuating exploitative and hostile relationships among ethnic groups than to enhancing the integrity of the disadvantaged ones.

The positive implication of this discussion is that the social health of the ethnic groups that comprise a city is strongly influenced by their roles in the economic life of the city. In particular, the social health of a group seems to require that there be some significant markets in which its members occupy influential, if not dominant, positions. Surely the Negroes are distinguished from the other ethnic groups in precisely this regard: that they have no such economic bases of power, status, and social mobility.[4] If this be so, effort should be concentrated on creating such economic foundations for social health for the Negro communities. I am well aware of the difficulties of this enterprise, and I am struck also that none of the major programs with which I am acquainted are pointed in this direction, which may be the essential one.

[4] See St. Clair Drake, "The Social and Economic Status of the Negro in the United States," *Daedalus,* vol. 94 (fall, 1965), pp. 791–814, and Eugene P. Foley, "The Negro Businessman: In Search of a Tradition," *Daedalus,* vol. 95 (winter, 1966), pp. 107–144, both in the *Daedalus* symposium on the Negro American.

Criteria, Institutions, and Function in Urban Development Decisions

Kenneth J. Arrow

Harvard University

Theme

The usually stated criteria for urban renewal or planning decisions refer to the welfare of an abstract organism, the city, rather than that of concrete individuals. I will argue here that the application of this organismic criterion can easily lead to inefficiency and that any redistributional effect implied by it is likely to be perverse, that is, from the poor to the rich. The proper criterion is essentially the national income modified by a positive weight for redistribution of income downward.

However, I further suggest that the ready acceptance of the organismic criterion has behind it some implicit understanding of two very real factors which in practice operate as constraints on optimization: (1) institutional restrictions on taxation, in particular the reliance on property taxation, which implies that increase in the economic value of the city permits increase in the welfare of its concrete inhabitants; (2) the increasing returns character of the city as a productive unit, at least in some of its aspects, which also implies that measures benefitting the city as an entity increase efficiency in production. I suggest, though, that better analysis would explicitly recognize these conditions as constraints rather than absorb them into the criterion function. In the first place, they are only one set of factors, to be weighed against others, and in the second place, when recognized explicitly, they may suggest other policy measures than simple improvement of the city as such; for example, alternative means of taxation and possible increased emphasis on "new towns."

The present discussion is intended to refer to industrial and commercial, as well as residential, use of land.

The Organismic Criterion

Much policy discussion implies that the aim is the benefit of the "city," as an organism or even a geographical area. For a long time there was a general view that benefits were attached to a piece of land; an improvement in its value or in the value of the buildings placed on it or, in some instances, in its aesthetics was regarded as the condition for the existence of benefits for the community. The effect on those previously living in the area (typically, low-income classes) or on those elsewhere in the city facing increased competition for housing space was ignored.

Popular pressure—in this case rather in advance of the economists—has compelled at least some attention to the problem of relocation (though, I suspect, the direct concern with relocation probably leads to inefficient means of dealing with the underlying problem of housing costs in the city). But variant versions of the same fallacy of attaching values to places rather than people still persist. Policies are openly addressed to inducing the migration of upper- and middle-income classes to the city and, less openly, to driving out lower-income classes and especially blacks, or at least to preventing their further in-migration. The convenience of the freeway as a barrier circumscribing the expansion of the ghettos and protecting middle-class neighborhoods from the disutilities of contact with a negatively valued way of life has been observed by city planners. More rigid enforcement of health and housing codes may have a similar effect. There also appears to be a certain amount of popular discussion of policies designed to make the city more attractive in various ways to middle-and high-income groups, such as better provision of cultural facilities. The aim of all this might be described as the maximization of per capita income of those who live in a certain geographically described area even though no individual is better off.

The Efficiency Criterion

The city is really a strange entity for optimization purposes. The city is not a particular set of people; they move in and out. Any political decision made in a city has spill-in and spill-out effects. The only meaningful national criterion for urban policy is the maximization of national income modified by distributional considerations. The latter clause should mean redistribution in favor of lower-income groups and victims of discrimination, not in favor of higher-income groups as might be inferred sometimes from the allocation of public expenditures. Orthodox benefit-cost analysis is applicable, which means that improvement in the efficiency with which services are supplied is the primary criterion for urban renewal and other planning activities.

To meet an obvious objection, efficiency should properly be measured with regard to the creation of all values, tangible and intangible. For all the usual textbook reasons, a benefit need not be measurable in the marketplace. Amenity values are to be included. But it must be admitted that there is a chance of class bias entering here. Aesthetic considerations are more apt to be recognized and demanded as public goods by those whose leisure and education enable them to appreciate such considerations. In the absence of a good system of benefit taxes or of sufficient progressivity in the general tax structure, the general recognition of amenities may be distributionally perverse even though efficient.

Two Implications of the Efficiency Criterion

1. In the evaluation of efficiency, the test of the market is, of course, very important, though, for well-known reasons, not necessarily conclusive in all aspects. A classical example of

market failure in the urban development area is the need for land assembly. Because of increasing returns to scale in manufacturing or commerce, or of neighborhood effects in housing or public centers, the development of a large area of contiguous land under single control may be necessary for efficiency (in the wide sense, including intangibles). Because the land is currently held in small parcels, most of which are indispensable to the proposed project, the acquisition of the land on the private market may be unduly costly because each seller can attempt to realize the entire surplus to be created by the project. (Each seller has monopoly power, and the competitive assumptions that imply the efficiency of the market solution are far from being realized.) Here is an instance in which the government should use its coercive power to acquire the land at the market price that would prevail in the absence of the proposed project and to ensure that the land is used for the proposed project (either by resale or by the government's own use of it).

But efficiency does demand that the value of the assembled land in its new use be greater than the market value in its old use. Thus if the land is being used for commercial or industrial purposes, the sale price of the assembled land should exceed the cost; the government should make a profit (there is no reason to make a gift of this profit to the developer). If the land is being used for residential purposes, part of the new value may be intangible, not measurable on the market. In this event, the efficiency criterion is that the loss, if any, on the resale or rental[1] of the land should be exceeded by the intangible values plus whatever benefits are derived from income redistribution (in subsidized public housing). It appears that in many instances the assembled land is sold at a considerable loss.

2. As noted earlier, there is great concern over the suburban migration of the middle classes. The efficiency criterion suggests that this is not a relevant problem in its most obvious aspects. The migrants are better off, as revealed by their ac-

[1] For a public housing project, the rental on the land is understood to be the difference between housing rents and the sum of current operating costs and interest, and depreciation on the capital used in construction. It is, of course, the capitalized value of these land rents which is to be compared with the original land cost to define the loss. Similarly, the intangible values and redistribution benefits are also to be capitalized.

tions. Any policies designed to bring them back or prevent their further migration are perversely redistributional.

The only legitimate arguments from the efficiency point of view must be based on externalities or on increasing returns. In the first class, the important point is that the efficiency justification of special policies to attract the middle classes must be based on advantages to the poor. Some of the arguments advanced are fallacious; some are in principle correct, though their quantitative importance remains to be established. An example of a fallacious argument is that a good deal of industry is relatively footloose and locates near where executives choose to live. Factually, of course, this argument is correct, at least in identifying one locational factor, but it has no implications for interventionist policy. The movement of industry with the location of executives is a pure transfer with no allocative significance.

A second argument is that the quality of municipal government is affected by the educational and social level of the voters and of the supply of public officials. This is sometimes argued most strongly with respect to the educational system; the middle class presumably demands quality and is willing to pay for it. Against whatever validity there may be to this argument must be offset a position taken by many observers, beginning with Lincoln Steffens: the values sought by a middle-class electorate may not be those of the lower classes, so that the higher middle-class efficiency in government is not necessarily efficiency in the directions relevant to the lower classes.

A third argument is that personal interaction between middle and lower classes is beneficial to the latter, presumably by setting examples and raising aspiration levels. This argument has been advanced most strongly with regard to education; the direct mingling of school children with different class backgrounds is supposed to improve the performance of the lower-class children (the Coleman Report is the latest documentation of this viewpoint).

Finally, still another argument frequently given is based on increasing returns rather than externalities. It is argued that cultural amenities require for support a large interested public, and this can only come from the middle classes. The necessary size is perhaps not so obvious: Athens in its classical period had a population little bigger than San Jose, and presumably a much lower per capita income, even allowing for tribute payments.

The quantitative importance of these valid arguments cannot, of course, be assessed without more empirical evidence than is easily available. For a long time to come the acceptance of policies based on these arguments will be a matter of judgment. But it is important to analyze them correctly to ensure both that the judgments are made about the right arguments and that the policies adopted actually realize the correct aims. Thus, attracting the middle class into the city by creating a superior portion of the educational system devoted only to middle-class students could not be justified by any valid efficiency argument.

The Policy Implications of Institutional Constraints: The Property Tax

So far, the efficiency argument has implicitly presupposed that the government disposes of enough instruments to achieve an efficient allocation of resources; but in fact governments in general have available only limited ranges of instruments, and the limitations on municipalities are especially severe. The city government is a provider of public services that have become extremely expensive because an affluent society demands more of public as well as other services. For reasons of convenience and precedent, the primary means of raising the needed resources is the real property tax.

As is well known in welfare economics, when the range of the government's instruments is restricted so that fully efficient solutions are unavailable, we are forced to resort to a "second-best" solution in which many of the familiar efficiency conditions are no longer valid. It is suggested here that much of the emphasis on increasing the value of property (rather than the welfare of people) finds some motivation as a second-best solution.

With a real property tax, any development that increases the volume of real property increases the tax base and, therefore, the possible supply of municipal services. Since the supply of land is fixed, this means that the city has an incentive to see increased building, even when not justified by the test of the market. The restriction to a real property tax thus appears to be a major creator of adverse incentives to the city government. The situation is especially ironic since the building tax, like any excise tax, creates a distinct welfare loss and in particular does so by discouraging building. The city thus makes up by subsidies in particular instances for the adverse incentives created by its general tax structure.

This situation suggests the need for a serious two-pronged research effort into (1) the use of a genuine price system for municipal services to the extent possible (no doubt limited but surely more extensive than at present) to reduce the dependence on the real property tax;[2] and (2) the replacement of the real property tax by a pure land tax. The land tax has been a favorite of theoretical welfare economists for a good many years because of the absence of disincentive effects; perhaps it is time to see what its conditions and impact would be in practice. Note that if labor and capital were perfectly mobile, the "going value" of a city would be reflected exclusively in its land values (except to the limited extent that it appears as prices paid for municipal services). The mobility of capital is probably a reasonably valid assumption, but there are locational preferences that impede the mobility of labor. As a result, the city as a going organization creates consumers' surpluses which are also subjects for taxation. It is, at any rate, widely believed that much of this surplus is received by suburban residents, with obvious implications for taxing.

Increasing Returns and the Functions of a City

From the economist's viewpoint, the existence of the city and the argument for its preservation are the result of a compound of externalities and increasing returns, usually referred to as "agglomeration effects." They are difficult to isolate but are undoubtedly real. But today much popular and official opinion throughout the world is concerned with the

[2] The best analysis I know of is by W. S. Vickrey, "General and Specific Financing of Urban Services," *in* H. G. Schaller, ed., *Public Expenditure Decisions in the Urban Community* (Washington, D.C.: Resources for the Future, 1963), pp. 62–90.

possibility of excessive concentration in metropolitan areas (not necessarily central cities). This could in principle be explained by the fact that, because of deficiencies in the price system (not easily remediable), the individual bears the average rather than the marginal cost of congestion.

The existence of increasing returns can be an argument for policy to preserve and strengthen the city as an organism, since such a development will then entail increased efficiency. But if it were in fact true (which it may well not be) that the largest metropolitan areas are encountering diseconomies of scale, then the policy implication is rather different. Increasing returns may then appear as the obstacle to the creation by the free market of new metropolitan areas which will relieve the congestion of the old and thereby increase overall efficiency. If this situation obtains, government intervention is much more justified for the creation of "new towns" than for the preservation of the old.[3]

[3] One final reflection, rather loosely related to the foregoing. When dealing with a collection of highly durable capital goods, it may easily be optimal to go through cycles of growth and (relative) decay. As a capital good (house, factory) gets older, its efficiency declines, at least relative to the newest capital goods; but there will be a long period in which it is not profitable, privately or socially, to replace it with new goods. A perfectly balanced growth is almost impossible to achieve and, in general, need not be desirable. If there are agglomeration economies up to a point, and diseconomies of scale beyond, then optimal policy calls for rapid initial growth, implying the existence of a large block of obsolescent capital at some later point of time. Continued growth at a constant rate will keep the proportion of "blighted" areas constant but will be undesirable because of the diseconomies of large scale.

Decentralization and Urban Programs

Julius Margolis

Stanford University

Historically, the organization of activity in the metropolis conformed closely to the dominant themes of American economic and political ideology: the market was seen as the preferred instrument; and, if it proved imperfect, the local government was expected to try to correct its shortcomings. The repeated crises of the metropolitan areas—congestion, crime, pollution, racial disorders, fiscal inadequacy, slums—have led to a dilution of the principles of decentralization. The market has been constrained and manipulated in innumerable ways: local officials have increasingly turned to the state capitals and Washington for financial and technical help; the shift of responsibility to government and within government to higher levels has not been without resistance, but the trend is clear. Less clear are the reasons for the trend and, possibly more important, whether the growing importance of the national government necessarily implies centralization of authority and administration in place of market exchanges and local decision-making.

The analysis of centralized administration versus decentralized markets in urban programs raises far more questions than we can cover here. We shall focus on issues we believe are most relevant to the themes of creative federalism in the context of federal urban programs; therefore, we shall overstress the relations among governments, recognizing that the more important policy issues are the relations between government and private parties.

Institutional Decision-Making Structures

Solutions of urban problems always involve an institutional decision-making structure, which specifies the rules of behavior and interactions among the individuals and organizations, and thereby the likelihood of achieving the proposed solution. Whatever is the social preference for the optimal allocation of resources, its realization is dependent upon behavior of individuals seeking to reach goals, as they privately define them, subject to technological and social constraints. One of the most insightful ways to understand a policy or program is to view it as a complex interaction of decision-makers. One organizational extreme would be a centralized structure with a single decision-maker, where there would be government-imposed programs with no initiative left to private parties except to emigrate; at the other extreme would be complete decentralization where everyone would be a decision-maker, and the government would be restricted to preventing physical coercion among private parties while the individuals and organizations would be free to contract among themselves.

The components of the organization of an urban area include households, firms, governments, and nonprofit groups. These units are linked via market and nonmarket exchange, political, legal, psychological, and social relations. Policy formation and implementation in the area of urban programs involve all of these types of interactions. No wonder analysts have felt helpless before the complexity of the problem, especially as poorly understood racial relationships have become increasingly important and have come to affect all other linkages. In this paper I shall concentrate on formal relations dealing with social control. We can distinguish between horizontal and vertical links: horizontal links connect units where authority is absent, while vertical links imply the existence of authority. I will restrict the discussion to the vertical structure, though it is clear that behavior in the horizontal sector will seriously affect any outcomes.

The view of a hierarchy of decision-makers suggests that we distinguish between two types of decisions and two dimensions of a structure of decision-makers. The two types of decisions are substantive and coordinative; the two dimensions of a structure are the organization of information and the control and diffusion of authority.

A *substantive decision,* in its pure form, is a direct order of resources to perform certain acts. In contrast, a *coordinative decision* is a set of orders or rules to affect the behavior of other decision-makers. In practice, most decisions are a composite of both, but the distinction is still useful. In a vertically linked structure of decision-makers, the higher levels are likely to be making coordinative decisions and the lower levels, substantive ones. For instance, consider a class of decisions dealing with the substantive: the higher level's allocation among lower levels does not directly call for the movement of resources, while the expenditures of the lower level would be purchases of resources. In a completely centralized system where the lower levels spent according to a manual of instructions composed by the center, the allocational decisions of the center would be both coordinative and substantive.

Of more concern to us are the two dimensions of decentralization: *information* and *authority.* Because the confusion of the two is troublesome, it would be best to use different terms. Let us refer to the distribution of authority as the *diffusion of authority;* and the distribution of information will be referred to as *organizational decentralization.* In some rough measure the differences between authority and information conform to those in price theory when we distinguish between equity and efficiency. The degree of desired diffusion of authority is a political decision; the degree of desired informational decentralization is an efficiency calculation.

We know from the theorems of price theory that a sharp distinction between equity and efficiency cannot be drawn, since every improvement in efficiency also carries with it implications for equity. Similarly every change in the structure of information will affect the diffusion of authority, so that there are no politically neutral revisions in decision-making structures, even though the intent may be to leave the diffusion of authority undisturbed.

We define authority as a relationship between a decision-maker and a delegate. If *B* uses *A*'s objective function in making his decision, we say that *A* has authority over *B* or that *B* is simply a delegate of *A*. We can conceive of two types of centralized system:

(1) *Authoritarian*—*A* does not issue orders to *B* nor does he audit the behavior of *B*. *B* acts as *A* would have done, if *A* were in *B*'s situation. The best example of this type of situation would be a highly authoritarian religious order where the dogma is interpreted at the center and followed by members. A less authoritarian structure would be a professional group, for example, medicine, which has a code of acceptable practice and can decertify or punish members if they violate that code. At the other extreme we have economists who can present completely opposite policy recommendations without loss of face in their profession.

(2) *Dictatorial*—If *B* acts on instructions provided by *A* and *A* prepares his instruction on the basis of information that is as complete as the information available to *B*, then we can say that *A* dictates to *B*. *B* is no more than an extension or agent of *A*. We suggest the peculiar condition that the dictator must have full information because without it he may find himself unduly influenced by the selective information forwarded by *B*. Many an agency head discovers that his "orders" are no more than endorsements of proposals sent up by his subordinates. Without knowledge of alternatives, he may find it impossible to issue directives.

The approval of an authoritarian system is implied in the acceptance of a dictatorial organization, but if *B* either does not know *A*'s preferences or acts according to his own preferences, or if he does not make available to *A* all of his information, then some degree of decentralization will be present. In practice, of course, *A*'s information will be incomplete, *B* will have private objectives, and, no matter how authoritarian or dictatorial the proposed organization, there will be some decentralization.

The impossibility of an authoritarian or dictatorial organization need not give much comfort to the advocates of decentralization. A fully decentralized system is just as unlikely. All societies have governments, and even judges demand extensive information before assigning blame and assessing damages. The question we face is how to design one organization to achieve an "optimal" distribution of authority and information.

In the context of the division of responsibility between federal and local governments, it is clear that a Federal Department of Urban Affairs would collapse under the burden of trying to administer the public sector of all urban areas. If municipal governments were all federalized, we would soon discover that variances from expected behavior would be very common. It is less clear that federal government must exercise some control over locals. A government over a metropolitan area may be advisable; but it is not obvious that it must be the federal government, though the intervention of more central authorities is understandable where there is no metropolitan government.

Centralization versus Decentralization

The debate about centralization or decentralization in urban programs centers around conditions associated with fiscal transfers from the federal to the local governments. The constitutional status of states, and thereby their subdivisions, ensures a substantial distribution of authority among the levels of government. Though a fully centralized system of urban management, comparable to the Post Office's administration of intrametropolitan communication, is unlikely, the federal manipulation of incentives and setting of constraints can go quite far in establishing a centralized system.

The model of the extreme centralized urban society would be one where the preferences of the central authority dominate and each acre is assigned a specific land use and each resident, a specific set of activities. Orders about detailed actions would flow from the center, and reports on the behavior of the units would flow to the center. At the other extreme of the spectrum, authority would be widely diffused, and the center would only establish rules for individual contracting. The instruments of extreme centralization are orders, and information flows to make them operative; the instruments of extreme decentralization are laws and judicial proceedings to enforce them. The mixed system is more interesting: though authority is dispersed, the perferences of the center have weight and the instruments, in addition to the above, would be an elaborate set of incentives available to the center to influence the behavior of the units. In the mixed urban organization, therefore, the center would establish rules of market behavior (constraints on alternatives), would issue orders (for example, housing standards), and would provide incentives (taxes and subsidies to change the costs and benefits of alternative private actions). All actual systems are mixed, but this says little, because there are profound differences among systems based upon the mix of controls used and the distribution of functions among levels of government. There are new towns that barely vary from the architect's plans drawn in the offices of the National Ministry, and there are squatters' precincts where the government exercises its authority only via the policeman on the beat.

Though orders, constraints, and incentives are used by the federal government in its relations to local governments, the last is the most common. Grants to locals have increasingly become the mechanism of influence. The power of the grant is that it changes the costs to the locals of following certain courses of action. Grants would seem to be a minimal form of centralization because the locals are not ordered to choose, but associated with the grant is a set of conditions which either constrain the locals from some actions or direct them to perform others. The result is not likely to be the most preferred from the perspective of either level of government: the national constraints are not likely to be most appropriate for the locals; and the center does not know the decision function of the locals, so the constraints and incentives will not be designed most effectively. Despite the many shortcomings of this instrument, it has the great advantage of flexibility; it permits many combinations of incentives and constraints. The philosophy of intervention underlying this transfer of authority has been pragmatic with the anticipated consequences that the resulting system is inefficient and possibly contradictory of policy objectives.

In Search of Optimal Decentralization

The support for decentralization arises from two sources: (1) Our society assigns a high value to decentralization in general and to a decentralized government in particular (that is, a decentralized system may be preferred to a centralized one even if the former is less efficient). (2) There is a widespread belief, not without foundation, that extended administrative structures are inflexible, cumbersome, and generally inefficient. The first interest is political, that is, it involves judgments about values held by different groups in society; the second interest is managerial in that there is less heed of values and more concern with effective operations. Again we must stress that one should not overstate the distinction between politics and administration.

The arguments for decentralization as an objective per se, not considering its administrative advantages, take two tacks: political participation and accessibility. We consider these arguments in terms of their direct benefits to individuals and benefits to the political system which are a public good.

Political participation as a consumer benefit is an important commodity. The political game is played by millions of persons for the sheer joy of meetings, debates, intrigue, and so on. It is unlikely to replace television or baseball; but some persons receive huge satisfactions from participation, and many persons receive some satisfaction. The greater the number of elections, the more widely dispersed the candidate and issues, the more likely will a random individual be involved and therefore moved to participate.

A more ennobling argument for political participation is its value as an investment rather than as a consumer good. The argument that the community participation programs of the O.E.O. have proved weak because the poor are not wise decision-makers is often countered with the claim that the poor who participated have received a private incentive to improve themselves and an education in political involvement. The participants, it is asserted, would become political leaders of the poor so that the political system will be more representative. Therefore, though the poor may not "enjoy" the political game, they will prove to be more astute participants in the future if they are given some responsibility today.

In practice the number of the poor, or of the citizens at large, who participate in politics is relatively small. Against the consumer benefits we should place the costs borne by individuals out of their sense of responsibility. There are many who find it burdensome to become familiar with candidates, attend meetings, and read literature, but who play the game out of a sense of duty and are prepared to support every measure to reduce the length of the ballot. For these reasons the magnitude of net consumer benefits is very uncertain.

Accessibility not only benefits the individual who, by appeal to the government, may be able to redress a personal wrong, but it also results in improved acceptability of government. An individual will have less information about how to appeal to a more distant government than to a local one. Improvements acceptable to all parties may not be made simply because the costs of a distant meeting are too great. In addition to the individual gains, we should consider the changed attitude of individuals toward the government. The recognition that an appeal is feasible may give the appearance that the government is less arbitrary, making people more willing to accept with good grace the acts of the more local government.

Against these positive features of accessibility, some negative features should be listed. In particular there is evidence that heterogeneous small governments tend to be frustrated. The political bargaining process is carried on most smoothly when not too exposed to the public so that the participants need not feel that they are always confronting the opposition. Further, the accommodation process of government cannot satisfy everyone; and, if each unhappy person had his day in court, the bureaucracy, as well as the elected officials, would be overwhelmed. Fears of opposition cause small governments to rely on a consensus before they act. As a result the status quo tends to be the preferred choice. The more distant the government, the higher the cost of griping, the more likely will the government act—its opposition is dispersed, invisible, and anonymous. The member of the planning commission of New York who grants a variance is not likely to live in the neighborhood and feel the wrath of his neighbors. This politically favorable feature of a more centralized system may seem to contradict the morality of democracy; but then all aggregation procedures in the political domain are nondemocratic, and, until we know more about the social processes establishing the power of the central authorities, it would be hazardous to conclude that they are less responsive to the public.

The more frequently discussed arguments about the optimal degree of decentralization are more technical: they deal with the same issues raised in the discussions of the failures of the market and with counterarguments dealing with the costs of administration. Though the arguments were developed in the context of government intervention in, or displacement of, private markets, they are equally applicable to the discussion of the centralizing of urban powers in the hands of the federal government. We shall discuss, in turn, the problems of objective functions, externalities, incentives, and information. Our major attention will be given to objective functions, but it is only because of shortage of space that we do not extend the remarks on the other issues, which are equally important.

Objective Functions

Analysts have found it impossible to devise an acceptable procedure by which to derive a social welfare function from an aggregation of individual utility functions. The same difficulties would confront the analyst if he were to try to aggregate "urban utility functions" to create a national urban welfare function. If we ignore the impossibility theorems of the welfare economists and deal with more operationally derived objective functions, other difficulties develop because the operational procedures by which "implicit objective functions" for cities are established are very different from those of the federal government. This difference gives rise to a basic conflict, and to some it poses a basic question of political philosophy. Let us consider the problem at two levels: the criteria for federal urban programs and the conflict of national and local operational criteria.

The most common national criteria are those of benefit-cost analysis. These say that the program should be designed so as to maximize the difference between the benefits and costs of the program. The benefits are the payments that the users of the program would be willing to pay if pricing were feasible; the costs are the value of the resources in other uses. Of course, there are difficulties in discovering the proper set of "prices," and the difficulties become even greater when we include distributional criteria; but the main point is that the basic rule suggested for the national government is the aggregation of individuals as consumers, not citizens, amended by a political judgment about distribution. The distributional amendment is not doctrine, since many would argue that the distributional goals can be handled better by taxes and transfer than by design of public programs.

The choice of the aggregation of individual consumer utilities as an objective can be contrasted with an objective function that contains as its arguments levels of public output, measured by program levels or by consumer characteristics. The relative levels of the programs are to be determined by political consultation of legislative, executive, and administrative leaders.

Illustrative entries in the objective function would be such quantitative targets as number of children in school, number of hospital beds, number of dwelling units constructed, and so on. It is difficult to associate the numbers resulting from this process with any normative values, but one might argue that there is a consensus about the process of political consultation and thereby the outputs of the process have a normative content. This argument could be strengthened if the bargainers had information about the benefits and costs of marginal adjustments in each of the service levels. Instead of the process leading only to political accommodation, it is possible that explicit statement of marginal benefits and costs might lead to a consensus about desirable tradeoffs among objectives and thereby weights to be assigned to objectives.

The defense of a political consultation process can be, and sometimes is, extended to the division of authority among levels of government. It is argued that the municipal government has local participation in legislative representation and in the many informal pressures that shape public opinion and the perception of public personnel. Though the local government is assumed to be responsive to the local community, it is argued that it is deficient in fiscal resources and, therefore, there is the need for the federal government to raise funds and to transfer them to the local government for local disposition. The local governments would be relied upon to design programs responsive to local demands and would be expected to administer them more efficiently because of their high local visibility.

An alternative use of locally derived objective functions would be more in line with programs of the Model Cities type where local officials are asked to be responsive to both their own preferences and a set of federal objectives. Community participation in planning is encouraged, but such planning must follow an elaborate set of federal guidelines. The processes of reconciliation are not clear in this instance. The current situation is highly unstable, and well-designed research may be very influential in formulating a new structure.

Of course, local political leaders and their allies in Congress are strong proponents of placing allocational authority in the hands of the locals. Each city considers its problem unique, and each wants to be free to design its own programs; but freedom of political and administrative maneuverability is neither a national nor a local goal.

Both of the above "decentralized" schemes rely heavily on the view that the locally defined objective functions should provide strong inputs into the final decisions. More centralized schemes, with little concern for local preferences, are typical of other programs. In these cases, we have categorical grants that must be spent in highly specified manners. It is still a degenerate decentralized scheme, as local officials have an option of spending or not; but if they choose to spend, then the rules under which they operate are comparable to the quantity and quality rules found in highly centralized planning schemes. Even here, except for the instances where the quantity and quality rules are so detailed that the programs are almost part of a federal bureaucracy (for example, state national guards), there exist local options, and local preferences play a contributory or disruptive role. Therefore, for all types of organizational structures ranging from policy decentralization with redistributional transfers to local administration of federally designed programs, local objective functions have a significant role. Relatively little is known about their characteristics and how they are related to federal programs.

Local objective functions, as revealed by the behavior of municipal governments, are heavily weighted toward site enhancement rather than toward resident welfare. Further, the definition of resident takes a peculiar form, probably understandable only by the dominance of a concern with *site* rather than *human* values. For instance, would a city encourage a facility (a housing project or medical center) that would increase the entry of low-income migrants who, while in the city, would greatly improve their productivity but who would move elsewhere as their income prospects approached the average of the community? The answer would be no, even though it is apparent from the national perspective that there is a great need for such facilities. An even more extreme example of "human indifference" can be seen in the argument that cities will "underinvest" in the children of their permanent residents if the children are likely to migrate. Thus, the welfare of their permanent residents might be reduced by the city's indifference toward their "family capital" which is located elsewhere and does not bring a money income to the city.

The site preference in local objective functions is derivable from the structure of political influence in the city. Bureaucratic structures in most municipalities are weak and highly visible to the citizenry. Local civil servants are paid low salaries. They are not highly professional, and, in general, they are not insulated from political influence. This vulnerability to influence would be considered a virtue by those who urge a reliance on local aggregation of individual utility functions, but two key questions arise: (1) How does the structure of local political influence affect local objectives? and (2) Does the aggregate of optimally specified local objectives result in optimal national objectives?

Political influence, like other goods, is available at a price. Outright corruption is an obvious market (the conditions under which corruption leads to improved allocations have not been studied; corruption is rarely seen as a consequence of an uncleared market and an exchange to clear the market), but there are many other more socially acceptable forms of influence that are subject to the market calculus. Contributions to political organizations, attendance at council or political meetings, informal talks with neighbors and friends, promises of favors, threats, even voting (especially if it includes acquiring knowledge about the debated issues) involve cost. Each individual will be prepared to bear these costs, and thereby enter into the process of determining the local objective function based upon his private calculation of the net benefits to him of the public decisions. Political involvement will be related to the individual surpluses in the city. For most persons, the surpluses are small because they move often; therefore, their demand for a site in a neighborhood or city is elastic, and this elasticity would extend to the public outputs. Firms with large fixed capital and landowners who have a large stake in rents have committed themselves heavily to the future development of an area, and they would be willing to invest heavily in political costs. The same argument would extend to immobile residential groups, for example, Negroes in the ghetto. With low income and high unemployment, their political costs would take the form of expenditures of time. This cost is a burden to the municipal officialdom rather than a payoff to them, but possibly equally effective.

The thrust of the above remarks is that the implicit objective function is likely to reflect the surpluses received by the less mobile groups. The dominant group will be the landowners and their associated business partners. Their payoffs need not be in social improvement of the residents, but a change in land use which might be adopted by exporting problem populations or by restricting their entry. If all communities pursued these objectives, not only would each community be frustrated, but in the process, the national goal of improvement of the impoverished would also be frustrated. National objectives are not the sum of the local objectives. There are countervailing forces: many businesses are national in scope and their leaders have perspectives beyond the city; banks have investments beyond a city; professional and bureaucratic groups have metropolitan and national associations with broad orientations; and, of course, individuals have their own utilities.

The above hypotheses about the political structure of locals and the implied objective functions are not based upon any solid empirical or analytical work. There are more descriptive studies on which to base hypotheses that can be empirically tested.

The ability of the local government to be the vehicle for the development of the local objective function is greatly reduced by the extensive degree of decentralization or fragmentation of local governments. One form of decentralization in the local areas of great relevance to urban programs is functional specialization among the locals. Schools are usually independent, welfare is handled by counties, water may be supplied by special districts, and so on. Clearly, there is a greater possibility of relating benefits and costs if there is a single government responsible for a function. Interestingly enough, advocates of an independent government praise its freedom from political influence, while those who regret the multiplicity of governments argue that it is necessary to have a unitary government to establish political responsibility.

There is usually less political interest in the independent governments, but beyond that, very little else is known. It is possible that functional specialization may mean insulation from local political influence since the specialized governments are usually nonpartisan; therefore, more power would go to the federal bureaucracy.

Another form of functional specialization is functional fragmentation, where there is a division of responsibility among overlying general governments. Counties may handle housing and welfare while the municipalities will handle the police functions associated with the neighborhoods. The city is the "politically responsible" authority to whom pressures are directed, but they may be misdirected if the allocational authority is in the hands of the countries, subject to state constraints. The typical structure has the welfare and housing functions located in county governments and the school authority separated from county and municipality.

Some kinds of decentralization are more akin to spatial fragmentation, but lead to socioeconomic class decentralization. The division of the territory of the metropolitan area into dozens of territorial governments has harmful consequences in terms of neglected externalities, but of more importance is the development of relatively homogeneous communities. Spatial goals of municipalities become identified with social class goals of homogeneous groupings. As a consequence, there will be underinvestment in public and urban facilities for the lower socioeconomic classes. Even though each community might welcome some improvements for the lower classes, none will make the move on its own. The simplest solution is for each territorial government to maintain its barriers via zoning and other land use controls, and to pay taxes to a central government to reallocate funds to the central city which houses the poor. This division has a persuasiveness about it. It characterizes the current situation; but it may prove to be a dismal failure if the spatial differentiation leads to difficulties in access to jobs and decent education.

Externalities

The weight of the arguments about the derivation of objective functions has tended to support decentralized systems; the opposite is true for externalities. In the sphere of the private economy, an externality is an effect that is not priced. It is an output the firm does not sell, or it is an input it does not purchase. Illustrations would be a hydroelectric plant that regulates stream flow in order to stabilize energy output but does not sell the improved navigation possibilities, or a plant that uses the river to carry away its wastes but does not compensate the fisherman whose sport is ruined. In the public sphere we can refer to externalities as benefits or costs that accrue to parties outside the jurisdiction of the relevant government or agency. The park for one city may enhance the amenities for the residents of another city; the industrial development of a city may create traffic hazards for another; an increase in the educational facilities may reduce crime costs, and so on.

The existence of externalities has been the most extensively studied aspect of decentralization. Most attention has been paid to spatial spillovers of benefits and costs and somewhat less to the problems of economies of scale. By economies of scale we refer to the fact that there are decreasing long-run costs for some public facilities so a joint development by two cities will be less costly than by each of them separately. Unfortunately, research in the area of externalities and scale economies has not been well organized in terms of policy. Theoretical investigations have been very advanced, cost studies have been undertaken for a few public facilities, but there have been very few empirical studies of externalities or empirical investigations of policy alternatives.

The existence of an externality is sufficient to signal a defect in the decentralized system, but it is not sufficient to indicate what type of central response is called for. If there is no reason to reject the objective functions of the local governments, possibly the only response called for by the externality is to change the rules or constraints so that the externalities become internalized. For instance, it is said that there are extensive spatial externalities in education because of our highly mobile population. This need not mean that we should establish a national educational system, but merely a transfer of taxes from labor importing areas to labor exporting areas so that the area producing the exported benefit will gain in proportion. Or the existence of economies of scale in water supply need not mean a metropolitan water authority but only that governments should be free to sell water in all markets and therefore one of the city systems will grow to take advantage of the decreasing costs. The simple solution of merely transferring the function to a higher level of government is simple-minded, but unfortunately it is often the simplest to adopt.

Alongside the United States ideology of free enterprise and decentralization there is an ideology of administrative rationality: the administrative hierarchy should be extended to confront the extended problem. For instance, the existence of externalities among the military arms was the most persuasive argument for increasing the power of the Secretary of Defense, and the extension of administrative control over a program where the externalities are internalized is considered one of the great virtues of the planning-programming budgeting system introduced in the Defense Department. Though it is usually clear that the pure decentralized system would not be advisable, a centralized administrative solution might also be unwise when we consider the costs of information and the incentives for intelligent decisions. An extension of the scope of administration to internalize externalities carries with it the burdens of centralized systems: heavy information costs and inappropriate incentive systems.

Incentives

The objective function contains a weighted set of objectives of the government. In contrast to this statement of a set of desirable outputs, there is a set of incentives for the decision-makers to exert themselves and to influence the choices they make. One might consider the objective function as the formally accepted aims of the government and an incentive system as the operational set of gains to the decision-makers and their agencies which motivate their behavior. If the incentive system is optimally designed, the decision-makers will act as though they considered only the objective function. If the incentives are inappropriate to the objective function, the agency or government will be acting as though another objective function was dominant.

Incentives can be viewed at two levels: personal and organizational. The major set of personal incentives are the system of wages and promotions; for organizations we have a more complex set of rewards and punishments, with growth and stability being the principal criteria. The distinction between the personal and organizational incentives becomes blurred when we consider the top managerial decision-making group of the agency. Their loyalties become attached to the organization, and they receive significant nonpecuniary rewards as the organization thrives.

An extreme comparison illuminates the problem of personal incentives. If an entrepreneur should find a technique to continue to supply the same product without any inputs, he would leap at the opportunity, because he would immediately become wealthy. If a bureaucrat saw the same possibility of eliminating his agency without any loss of public welfare, his rewards would be a gold watch, the hatred of his colleagues, and a transfer to another job where his colleagues will be highly mistrustful. His dedication to the social welfare might be strong enough to lead him to propose the dismantling of his unit, but the lessons he should draw from his incentives would indicate the contrary. The gains to him arise from the size of the operation he commands: the larger it is, the greater will be his income and prestige. His personal rewards are a function of inputs rather than outputs.

The problem of incentives is aggravated, like all other problems of decision-making, by the presence of uncertainty. Because in any system, no matter how centralized, some discretion remains with a delegate, the authority must give him power to interpret the environment and to act, but at the same time the authority is aware that there are private gains and divisional loyalties which will make it likely that the decision will not be the same as the one the authority would make. The authority tries to reduce this variance with managerial selection procedures and training, and similar devices to minimize the difference between the objectives of the organization and those of its individual decision-makers. The authority also establishes an elaborate control mechanism to audit the activities of the decision-makers. The unfortunate aspect of a control machinery is that the control personnel are more adept at checking whether the operating decision-makers acted in accord with instructions rather than with their response to new situations.

The more extensive the control machinery the less effective will be the incentives to perform outstandingly. Control emphasizes short-run errors and a record of compliance with instructions. Since performance is difficult to judge, especially performance associated with uncertainty and the long run, a history of short-term conformity becomes an easier way to judge the delegates than success in meeting new situations.

An extended administrative structure requires routine and conformity to rules and thereby discourages consideration of new alternatives that may prove to be disruptive. The incentive pattern rewards conformity and supports these "bureaucratic" tendencies. A major research task is the investigation of incentive schemes that would encourage innovation without at the same time destroying the virtues of the administrative structure, the internalization of externalities and the exploitation of economies of scale. There has been a small amount of research on the extreme solutions such as the introduction of market mechanisms and the decentralization of authority so that the decision-maker is more actively confronted by the politically organized body of users; a greater amount of research has been devoted to administration improvements, but it has not been policy-oriented.

We know very little about motivations of bureaucrats, their career lines, patterns of decision-making, and relations to the public and to elected officials. It is believed that the federal bureaucracy is superior to local bureaucracy. Clearly the federal bureaucracy is more professional and better trained. It is unlikely that scale phenomena explain the full difference, but they must play some significant role.

For instance, my impression is that urban planners are highly mobile; their careers advance by their being appointed to larger cities. It seems reasonable to assume that their sense of devotion to their job is modified by their desire to leave and possibly prove their ideas adaptable to a larger city. This same conflict would not exist in a large federal bureaucracy. But then the poor quality of local personnel is evident even in the largest cities where promotion possibilities for the capable are more than ample.

We know even less of the incentives for the elected official. Certainly he wants to be elected, but this is only one of the items entering into his utility function. It is too simple to say that he exploits his elected post for private gain, because public acknowledgment of his work for the common good is valued by many an official. What are the differences in the motivations of city councilmen, state legislators, and congressmen? Strangely enough, little research has been done in this area, and none of it has been directed toward the implications for the distribution of functions among governments.

We have said little about incentives for organizations and instead we have stressed personal incentives. This emphasis was deliberate, to offset the imbalance that exists in the literature. The problem of centralization versus decentralization is to discover how decision-makers will function in alternative organizational systems, and for this we have to know much more about the individuals who will play the role of authorities or delegates.

Information

The issues in analyzing information flows are directions, magnitude, and substance—from whom, to whom, and about what—and how these flows are related to the structure of decision-making. The major factor, of course, is the cost of information, which can be subdivided into resources costs of processing the information, delay costs of waiting, and distortion costs each time a new person transforms or interprets the information. More information is available by increasing these costs, but this is not desirable if the additional costs are greater than the value of the additional information.

In a centralized system, if the center is to exercise its authority fully, the information flow will be huge. To economize the flow will be rationalized: information will be coded, standardized, condensed, limited. The problems that arise are severalfold. At this point it is impossible to code all of the uncertainties and contingencies that fill the minds of the observers who are close to the action. Second, the center will have reports standardized over many peripheral reporting units, and the codes may not be properly designed for any of them. Third, there is little certainty that the peripheral units report information to the best of their ability. If they know that the center's orders may be arbitrary or poorly informed, they may try to influence them by doctoring the information flow. Incentives are necessary to get men to report accurately, as well as to encourage them to act.

Clearly the functions to be performed by the center should be influenced by the feasibility of obtaining sufficient information for reasonable decisions. Though the presence of externalities may indicate the necessity or advisability of decisions being made at the metropolitan or even a national level, it does not follow that the center should make those decisions if the information should prove too costly.

There is a growing body of research on information systems for metropolitan areas. At this point my impression is that almost all of them accept the current pattern of operations as given and then try to develop more efficient ways to process data. Very little, if any, research is directed toward the relations between the distribution of authority and control and the costs of information.

Decentralization and Bureaucracy in Local Government

Irving Kristol

Editor, *The Public Interest*

The major story on page 1 of *The New York Times* for November 17, 1967, reported that the Model Cities Program was getting under way:

> The administration made public today a list of 63 cities . . . that will take part in the first phase of the model cities program. . . .
>
> . . . The winners will share $11-million in planning money appropriated by Congress last year. The exact amount of each grant will be worked out in negotiations between federal and local officials.
>
> After the cities have drawn up detailed plans and submitted them to Washington, they will become eligible for $300-million appropriated last month to carry out the rebuilding process.

At first glance, this looks all too familiar, a recipe for bureaucratic nightmare, after the fashion of the older urban renewal program, now generally thought to be something less than a success. You will have a small group of experts in the sixty-three cities—men who will, for the occasion, be presumed to be highly knowledgeable about slum life, slum people, slum buildings, slum real estate, and so on—trying to come up with a blueprint they can sell to their local constituencies and to their Washington overseers. You will have a smaller group of presumed experts in Washington working desperately to make sense of the detailed plans submitted to them, hoping against hope that the plans will actually be carried out as intended, worrying endlessly (and legitimately) about whether the reports they are receiving "from the field" have any connection with what is really happening. Very few of the experts will, of course, be expert enough to avoid major miscalculations. And even if they were, there would still be the delays imposed by bureaucratic red tape to throw their calculations into disarray. In short the Model Cities Program appears to be a typical social welfare program that threatens to metamorphose into one controversial shambles after another.

Only, in this case, there is something new. The men who devised the Model Cities Program were alert to the problems of bureaucratic mismanagement. They therefore wrote into the law a provision for "popular participation" in this bold new venture into city planning. To get its allotted funds, each of these sixty-three cities must demonstrate to Washington's satisfaction that citizens' governing boards in the affected neighborhoods "participated actively in planning and carrying out" the program. These boards are now being formed via popular election. In Atlanta, a white neighborhood has elected a couple of Ku Klux Klansmen. In Detroit, in a half-Negro, half-white neighborhood, the board is all-Negro. Officials in Washington are reported to be very upset at the way things are going.

Which leads one to contemplate the possibility that there is more than one kind of bureaucratic nightmare—and that the worst kind may yet turn out to be of the "antibureaucratic" variety.

The Right Problem at the Wrong Time

Americans have never taken questions of public administration too seriously. To do so is to suggest that there may be inherent limitations on the execution of the popular will (and our democratic ideology discourages such a notion), or that the natural capacities of the average American may be inadequate to the detailed tasks of government (a national heresy since the days of Andrew Jackson). But the experience of liberals during the Kennedy administration was a critical one. Whereas they had previously scoffed at criticisms of "bureaucracy"—by conservatives in general, and businessmen in particular—they soon discovered that there really was such a thing and that its power to thwart or distort social programs was never to be underestimated. Just as most intellectuals only get interested in education when their children start going to school, so the liberal intellectuals around John F. Kennedy suddenly found themselves getting interested in public administration when they discovered that their good ideas and fine intentions got mangled on the way to achieving reality.

The simple fact, they learned, is that the number of programs the political and sociological imagination is capable of inventing always exceeds the number of available people who can realize these programs *as intended*. You always end up with programs being carried out by a bureaucratic hierarchy that understands them only imperfectly and possibly may not even be much interested in them at all.

So it became proper for liberals to talk about the problems of "bureaucracy" and of "centralization," and many started doing so. As a matter of fact "decentralization" has, in general, become a very fashionable idea. Thus, where political scientists used to argue that municipal government was incapable of coping with the problems of the city and that larger, more comprehensive metropolitan governments were needed, this argument has suddenly been reversed. In his recent presidential address to the American Political Science Association, Robert Dahl pointed out that the population of New York City is about the same as that of Sweden, and that New York is "badly in need of being broken up into smaller units for purposes of local government." Indeed, Professor Dahl took a dim view of any unit of local government that encompasses more than 200,000 souls.

So far, so good. We have become keenly aware—and it's about time, too—of the deficiencies of overly centralized planning and overly centralized government. We are all decentralists now. But, unfortunately, liberal intellectuals do seem to have an uncanny knack for focusing on the right problem at the wrong time, and in the wrong way. They have opted for decentralization with the same kind of enthusiastic abstractness they once brought to centralization. They have slighted, when they have not entirely ignored, the supreme political consideration—circumstance. For, as Edmund Burke long ago observed, "Circumstances . . . give in reality to every political principle its distinguishing colour and discriminating effect. The circumstances are what render every civil and political scheme beneficial or noxious."

I shall have something to say later about the most significant "circumstance" that today affects (or should affect) our efforts at decentralization; but, first of all, it is worth taking a look at the way the *idea* of decentralization became the *ideology* of decentralization.

Populism and Neopopulism

We have, during this past decade, witnessed a mounting anxiety about the fate of democracy in a mass, industrialized society. We have simultaneously witnessed a sharp upsurge of populism in American feeling, both on the left and (to a somewhat lesser extent) on the right. A "credibility gap" has emerged which separates the citizen, not merely from any particular administration, but from government itself. As a result, the need for "visible government" (in New York Mayor John Lindsay's phrase) and the importance of "participation" (in just about everyone's phrase) has become widely accepted among social critics and social reformers. The vision of the American people regaining a lost political heritage through a revival of the "town meeting" within our large urban centers has become exceedingly attractive. And, since there is no blinking the fact that ours is a complex and interdependent society, the constituency for such "town meetings" is frequently redefined along "functional" lines, so as to transcend mere locality and encompass all those involved with one governmental program or another. Has not Sargent Shriver roundly announced that "welfare without representation is tyranny"?

At about the same time, various sociologists, psychologists, anthropologists, and social theorists came to the conclusion that conventional populism was not enough. The people had not merely to be "involved" or "consulted" so as to gain their active consent. The people had to "participate" in their democracy in a very special way, that is, through "social conflict." What these social critics had in mind was no reconstituted

New England town meeting of any kind: *that* was a vehicle for consensus. Rather, they entertained images of mass picketing, rent strikes, organized boycotts of local merchants, harassment of all official bureaucracies, and so on. Activities such as these, it was insisted, were necessary to the mental health and spiritual uplift of the people, and especially the poor and dispossessed among them.

Just where this particular ideology came from, and how it achieved its popularity, is an interesting question but, for our purposes, an irrelevant one. (Obviously, it had more to do with an initial animus against the status quo than with any ripe sagacity about the difficulties of public administration in a large democracy.) In any event, it came to be accepted by many eminent authorities and respectable institutions. The Ford Foundation has been a leader in stimulating this novel version of populism. A group of scholars at the Columbia School of Social Work has also played a notable role in sponsoring a neopopulist rebellion against "the welfare establishment." The New Left has made it clear that, in its eyes, "participatory democracy" was essentially connected with the class struggle. And black nationalism in the ghettos has learned to insist that true democracy is essentially connected with race conflict, and indeed is quite simply black power.

The whole business has by now become a thoroughly confusing tragicomedy of errors. And no group has been more confused than our governing authorities. Congressmen who voted for community action programs and all sorts of "maximum participation" clauses, thinking they were striking a blow against "bureaucrats" and in favor of "the grass roots," are beginning to wonder what they have wrought. In desperation, they resort to the only kind of defensive action they can think of: indiscriminately cutting the budget for social services.

The Schools of New York

Meanwhile, the impulse to decentralization, oblivious to its own ideological muddle and blind to circumstance, gathers momentum. The most sensational venture of the "new decentralization" is the Ford Foundation's program for turning over New York's public schools to locally elected school boards.

This is not the occasion to go into a detailed critique of the Ford plan. Suffice it to say that, in my opinion, and it is not mine alone, Ford's plan will drive white parents out of integrated (that is, mixed) neighborhoods, white children out of public schools, and white teachers out of the city altogether. It will have the same effect on many middle-class Negroes. In addition, it will certainly result in inferior education for Negro children in the central city, as experienced white teachers move (or are moved) elsewhere. All this will be accomplished in the name of "decentralization" and "neighborhood self-government," which, in reality, will mean school boards that polarize and intensify all latent racial and political conflicts in any particular section of the city.

It is conceivable—let us even say it is probable—that, had the Ford program been introduced fifteen or twenty years ago, it would have represented an improvement. At that time, the politics of the Negro community centered around the demand for "integration," and Negro leaders would have had considerable latitude in negotiating with whites over the manner and matter of education. This is no longer true. The dominant political ethos of the Negro community is now black nationalism.[1] So far as one can see, this ethos will become stronger rather than weaker in the troubled years that lie immediately ahead. This being true, the popularly elected school boards are going to be forums for conflict and hostility rather than cooperation and communality. They are going to be weak and turbulent authorities, not strong and resolute centers of direction. (Indeed, where such school boards already exist, on an advisory basis, this is precisely what is happening.) And if, after the initial turmoil and chaos, they should become strong and resolute, they are very likely to behave in a thoroughly racist way.

Decentralization Confused with Democracy

To criticisms of this kind, which have been directed against its plan for reorganizing public education in New York, the

[1] I am not saying that the majority of Negroes are, or ever will be, black nationalists—except perhaps in a highly attentuated and rather passive way. But it seems clear that no Negro group will be able to *oppose* black nationalism without committing political suicide. The antinationalists are already in the process of being transformed into "moderate" nationalists.

Ford Foundation has only one strong rejoinder: the present system doesn't work. It would be more accurate and more candid to say that the system "works" no less well than it ever did, but that it has not been able to cope with lower-class Negroes as it previously coped with, say, lower-class Italians. (Essentially the same thing can be said about our welfare system.) Still, it is clear enough that New York's public education system, even when and where it works, is very efficient in enforcing petty regulations, extremely inefficient in coping with new problems or new opportunities. There is indeed, then, *in the abstract*, a valid case for decentralization. But, even in the abstract, what kind of decentralization?

It is always a good idea, when reforming an institution or a program, to take guidance, not only from general principles or preconceived opinions, but from comparable institutions and programs that do seem to work. Now, not all of education in New York City is out of popular favor. The affluent private schools, on the whole, are well regarded by parents, students, and teachers. So are the anything-but-affluent parochial schools, which the majority of Negro parents would be delighted to send their children to, were there room for them. What is it that makes these schools acceptable at the least, desirable at the best?

The answer has nothing to do with these schools being run on principles of local democracy, which they are not. It has everything to do with these schools being run on principles of *delegated authority*. Specifically, the reason these schools "work" better is that they are governed by headmasters who have considerable managerial power, managerial discretion, managerial immunity to outside pressures (*including* parental pressures). From what I have seen of public school principals in New York City, they compare favorably enough to private school headmasters. What they lack is any kind of real power to do a good job.

I am not unaware of the difficulties involved in conceding to them this power. Indeed, the difficulties are just about identical with those the Ford Foundation program is likely to encounter, but with the tumult swirling around the choice of principal instead of the school board. In any case, I am not here interested in arguing the case for one particular kind of educational reform as against another. I wish only to stress a significant, and frequently misconceived, point: decentralization is one thing, democracy is another. The government of

Sweden is far more decentralized than the government of New York City, but it is not thereby more democratic. Indeed, the Swedish government is probably less democratic than is New York's—and governs better.

Or, to put it another way: *decentralization, if it is to work, must create stronger local authorities, not weaker ones. Effective decentralization does not diffuse authority; it takes the power that is diffused throughout a large bureaucracy and concentrates it into new nuclei of authority.* Before we commit ourselves to any scheme of decentralization, we ought to make certain that this particular reconstitution of authority is what we really want. And I find it instructive to note that many of those who favor radical decentralization of education in our northern urban regions are simultaneously demanding the extension of federal bureaucratic controls over education in the South.

The Most Important Circumstance

In the United States today, the key circumstance that ought to affect one's attitude toward decentralization is the relationship between black and white—the present racial tensions we dare not ignore, the future integration we dare not despair of. Every reforming enterprise must, first of all and above all, take its bearings from this circumstance. It is always useful to inquire to what extent we can decentralize our cumbersome service bureaucracies (in education, welfare, housing, perhaps even policing); but it is even more useful to inquire to what extent we can decentralize our services *without fractioning our heterogeneous political community.* I am not saying that, under present circumstances, such decentralization is always undesirable. I am saying simply that we must always ask *whether* it is, in the light of these circumstances.

Indeed, were it not for the racial heterogeneity of this nation, the organization of our social services would be a relatively superficial problem. Politicians, of course, might kick up a big fuss about one thing or another; but whichever way the issue was resolved, it wouldn't make all that amount of difference. Take education, for instance. To begin with, were it not for the race issue, it might not be widely regarded as a problem at all. (In the all-white neighborhoods of Brooklyn, Queens, and Staten Island, there isn't even as much dissatisfaction with the New York public school system as, in my opinion, there ought to be.) Second, if one wished to experiment with various forms of decentralization, one easily could; whatever controversies they engendered would not be more damaging than, say, present controversies in smaller communities over local school board issues. (In these controversies, feelings run high, but only temporarily.) Third, one could even contemplate experimenting with quite radical reforms that go beyond decentralization, such as extending consumer sovereignty to the educational sector by abolishing free schools and distributing educational expenditures (in either cash or vouchers) to parents, who could then shop for schools as they please. The important thing is that, whatever was tried or not tried, whatever worked or didn't work, would not seriously affect the shape of the American republic or its ultimate destiny.

But we *are* a racially heterogeneous nation. And we *are* committed to creating a racially integrated society.[2] This fact and this commitment are, and ought to be, dominant in our minds. It is therefore of great importance that the major impulses toward decentralization now come from the white segregationists in the South and the black nationalists (together with their white, radical allies) in the North. Should these impulses prevail, the task of molding this country into one nation will be made infinitely more difficult, and perhaps impossible. The statesman's responsibility is to resist these impulses where he can, to contain them where he cannot resist.

[2] One of the arguments of those who propose decentralization along racial lines is that "integration" is turning out to be a will-o'-the-wisp, anyway. I think these people have an erroneous and highly utopian notion of integration. Yes, of course the proportion of all-Negro or predominantly Negro schools is increasing in our central cities, as the Negro population of these cities grows. This is inevitable. But I would argue that this is a stage in the process of integration, rather than some kind of contrary tendency. The Irish, the Italians, and the Jews also flooded their local schools, in their time. Integration doesn't mean instant assimilation. It doesn't mean—has never meant in America—that a new ethnic group is going to be warmly welcomed into the bosom of the old. It means, to begin with, the establishment of a checkerboard pattern of ethnic neighborhoods, and many Negro "neighborhoods" are now emerging in different sections of New York City, for instance. (We mindlessly persist in calling them all "ghettos," but many people who live there don't think of them as such. After all, even in Bedford-Stuyvesant some 15 percent of the residents are homeowners.) Every day, and in almost every way, New York City is becoming much more "mixed up" racially than it used to be. Decentralization can freeze the pattern and reconvert neighborhoods back into ghettos.

Decentralization, in practice, has come too often to mean the hasty appeasement of these tendencies.

The School as Scapegoat

There are two further, and not unimportant, points to be made:

(1) *Decentralization is not likely to solve any of the problems of education in our northern ghettos.* The sociological evidence seems to be conclusive that the schools themselves have only a partial, maybe only marginal, impact on broad educational achievements. What we glibly call the "problem of education in the ghetto" is probably little more than an aspect of the problem of poverty. Though a devoted, imaginative, and inspiring teacher can always make a difference, in any school, any time, there's not much point in asserting that what the ghetto needs is masses of such teachers: they don't exist in the mass. Nor is there any evidence that changes in the curriculum matter much; or new school buildings as against old; or even smaller classes as against larger ones. What does count is the environment, as established by home and community. The basic fact is that middle-class Negroes, living in middle-class neighborhoods (whether integrated or not), do *not* have a "crisis in education." Centering one's attention on the schools is an effective way of distracting one's attention from the far more important realities of poverty and discrimination.

One can understand why residents of the slums should be tempted to make the schools scapegoats for all of their frustrations. One can even understand, though with less tolerance, why government officials should join in this witch hunt, denouncing the schools for failing to achieve what no schools can achieve. But it is less easy to understand why social scientists in general should wish to participate in this demagogic campaign. Perhaps they do so for the same reason right-wing groups also tend to make the school a center of controversy: they feel impotent to engender controversy about anything else.

(2) *It is an accidental fact, but an important one, that our large and cumbersome bureaucracies, in such fields as educa-*

tion, welfare, and in the civil service generally, happen to play a crucial role in integrating large numbers of middle-class Negroes into American society. These bureaucracies are, in truth, the best-integrated sectors of American society. To this end, they work exceedingly well. Decentralization of these bureaucracies will almost certainly mean disintegrating them. We shall end up with only Negro teachers in Negro schools, only Negro police in Negro neighborhoods, only Negro social workers handling Negro clients, and so on. That, in my view, would be a major step backward. And I take it as a terrible irony that the idea of "separate but equal" should, fourteen years after the Supreme Court's *Brown* decision, became so dear to the progressive heart and mind.

Even among the various racial and ethnic minorities themselves, decentralization is already furthering conflict. In New York City, the antipoverty program is pitting Negroes against Puerto Ricans in open hostility, with each side claiming that the results of local elections to the governing boards of various agencies are "unrepresentative." And, indeed, since so few people take part in these elections, the consequences are bound to be haphazard. The city is trying to cope with this problem by issuing directives that set "correct" numerical ratios, according to race, creed, and color. Since neighborhoods are always changing their ethnic complexion, these directives are subject to constant, and mathematically refined, revisions.

Nor is that all. If this kind of apportionment is to continue, someone will have to decide *who* is black, white, or in-between. This is less simple than would appear at first sight. A group of Negro employees of New York's Community Development Agency have opposed a Negro candidate for the post of commissioner on the grounds he is "not really black." The group informed both the city authorities and the press that it reserved the right to define blackness.

I began this essay by suggesting that, at this time and this place, bureaucratic nightmares might not be the worst imaginable nightmares. I also believe that, if by some miracle these bureaucracies did not now exist, we should have to invent them, as an indispensable mechanism of racial integration. Come to think of it, if we *did* invent them, and gave them a fancy overall title (Office for Professional Equality?), we should probably flatter ourselves on having taken a great stride forward to the Great Society.

Decentralizing these bureaucracies remains a valid and important long-term objective; but in these times, under these circumstances, it is precisely the wrong objective.

The Reform of Urban Programs

Poverty, Dollars, and Urban Problems

Anthony H. Pascal

The Rand Corporation

Introduction

On a number of recent occasions D. P. Moynihan has asserted, to paraphrase roughly, that although the federal government clearly has a comparative advantage in the collection and disbursement of money, state and local governments are superior agents for the design and operation of specific programs. The obvious implications concerning decentralization of program management are drawn from this assertion. Whether or not Moynihan would be gratified by the position, such a statement seems to place him in the center of a surprisingly wide spectrum of people who have voiced similar sentiments. These range from Paul Goodman and the S.D.S. to Barry Goldwater and the Y.A.F.

I would like to argue that only the first half of the above paraphrase is demonstrably true, that is, that the federal government is efficient at collecting and disbursing money. Government, in general, is not very good at producing and distributing goods and services, lacking, as it does, the prod of commercial competition. The simple fact that local governments are closer to the scene is not, on net, a necessary advantage. For example, if it is true that producer interests tend to dominate consumer interests politically,[1] then this dominance is less costly at lower governmental levels. If state and local officials are relatively badly paid and high mobility in the population confounds the effects of subfederal program variations, then belief in the superiority of lower-level management must be seriously questioned. This is not to argue that federal administration is superior, but simply that *no* strong case has been made for governmental provision, as opposed to financing through government, where other mechanisms are available.

Thus the implication is that governmental direction of any kind ought, where possible, to be sharply reduced, though not the financial resources the government can provide. I think we have not done nearly enough thinking on where this administrative reduction might be applied and how alternatives to it might be arranged.

What We Face, What We Know, and Where We Want To Go

There are a number of broad concepts that all of us would probably include in his personal list of general social objectives. It is these, of course, toward which the various urban programs ought to be directed, though we might argue about the weights to be given individual items. The goals would probably include personal liberty, economic efficiency, equality (at least of opportunity), and social stability.[2] The use of such Fourth of July phrases as objectives does not get us very far; but neither are they completely useless, as I hope to show.

There are several additional objectives that seem to be receiving growing attention. In part, they are derivable from combinations of the above four. One is opposition to bureauc-

[1] Anthony Downs, *An Economic Theory of Democracy* (Chicago: University of Chicago Press, 1963).

[2] This last would probably command (increasingly?) less assent than the first three or, at least, the radical dissatisfaction now expressed with the basic structure of American society would have us believe so. Also, I have not listed subsistence, or starvation-prevention, as a goal, because within the United States this is an insignificant problem in terms of magnitude of resources required.

racy, per se. Bureaucrats are accused of being unfeeling, unperceptive, wasteful, self-serving, and authoritarian. These epithets, if accurate, may have either a Darwinian or a Parsonian genesis.

A second, related objective concerns the elimination of class or racial oppression by government and private groups. "End Welfare Colonialism," "Neighborhood Control of Schools," and "Ghetto Self-Development" are frequent rallying cries of the antiestablishment participatory democrats, for instance.

Members of a much larger, but not nearly so articulate, group would add still a different objective to the list. They would assert that work is good and dependency bad—for the soul, for the children, for the national moral fibre, or whatever. Each of us, except for those who believe that technological unemployment for all is just around the corner, would have to admit that pro-work/anti-dependency, per se, is as legitimate an objective as many others, although perhaps we would give it a rather low weight.

Turning from goals to facts, what are the salient characteristics of the current social environment in which these objectives must be pursued? I would suggest the following as preeminent:

1. Prejudice exists. Admitting that much of observed prejudice can be explained as a class, as easily as a racial, phenomenon,[3] it is certainly basic and pervasive in contemporary American attitudes and institutions. Dealing with prejudice as a taste which people are willing to pay to indulge[4] reveals some interesting programmatic possibilities, explored below.

2. Resentment by the minorities and the poor against prejudice and unfulfilled promises is growing and is ominous.[5] Programs that help achieve the objectives without generating further resentment need to be sought.

3. The power of public authorities over those who, in particular, are the intended beneficiaries of public largesse is proliferating. To the extent this is true and undesirable we should search for program options that feature freedom, independence, and voluntarism.

[3] See Nathan Glazer, introduction to *Studies in Housing and Minority Groups* (Berkeley and Los Angeles: University of California Press, 1960).

[4] See Gary Becker, *The Economics of Discrimination* (Chicago: University of Chicago Press, 1957).

[5] Ominous either because one fears insurrection and revolution, or because one fears reactive callousness or hysterical repression.

Program Implications

None of the programs discussed here is original with me. Rather I hoped that by packaging them I could illustrate their commonalities, complementarities, and consistencies. I will refrain from commenting here on the political feasibility of the individual items and thus restrict my skepticism as to their practical prospects to the end of the paper.

A note on economic efficiency: All of the programs suggested below are *technically efficient relative to the programs they would replace,* for a variety of reasons. Courses in freshman economics, for example, teach us that, dollar-for-dollar, gifts in cash are always *at least* as valuable to recipients as gifts in kind, and usually more so. Secondly, these programs tend to stress individual self-interest rather than appeals to good will in furtherance of social objectives. Third, most of them generate budgetary costs only if and when measured (if not in all cases, actual) progress toward some goal is being made.

Income Maintenance

If we really want less material inequality in the United States, income guarantees are clearly the answer. Among the variations that have been proposed, those doing least to damage work incentives and least to encourage the conception of children (for example, the federally administered negative income tax) are probably best.

I think also that we must face the fact that we are talking here about equality and not "adequate" incomes for the poor, which is rather meaningless and arbitrary. Why not simply adopt Victor Fuchs's proposal and fix a poverty standard which is always at one-half the current median income, adjusted for family size and location?[6] It is no less arbitrary than the poverty lines used now and has the advantage of keeping attention directed to the real issue.[7]

[6] See Victor Fuchs, *The Public Interest* (summer, 1967), no. 8, pp. 88–95.

[7] I would also opt for Harold Watts' iso-prop concept (*Journal of Human Resources,* II, 1) in which the weight for valuing a given increment in a household's income is a function of the household's initial position with respect to the established poverty standard and in which the weights trail off to zero at some point *above* the standard.

A Considerable Increase in Death Duties

Suspecting, as we do, that the work incentive effects of inheritance taxes are rather insignificant, increasing death duties appears to be a rather attractive route toward more equality in American society. By definition, of course, this has important intergenerational effects; and, although it treats only one aspect of wealth inheritance,[8] it would certainly bring equality of opportunity closer.

A System of Training Subsidies

If work is good, we ought to make it both easier to obtain and more rewarding for low productivity and disadvantaged workers. A very clever and appealing scheme for doing so is discussed in Lester Thurow's paper in this volume.[9] It advocates paying firms (and public sector organizations?) bonuses to hire the hard-core unemployed. Since the bonus has a finite time dimension, the employer could be expected to provide specific training to those for whom he receives a bonus, so that, at the end of the period, the worker's productivity would have been augmented to the point where his market wage is permanently increased. An advantage of the scheme is that it forces employers to pay (that is, forgo the bonus) to indulge whatever prejudice they may have against minorities, rustics, people with prison records, and the like. An employer who believes it is his work force or his customers who are prejudiced would be compensated by means of the bonus for losses resulting from those sources. The magnitude of the bonus, by industry and location, could be determined over time through the equivalent of a simulated auction among firms for rights to receive the bonus.

The existence of such a program would make a potential companion scheme even more attractive: to increase the quantity and quality of general training (that is, the kind that is transferable between firms and in which, therefore, the employer has little incentive to invest) by issuing training vouchers to the hard-core unemployed which would be usable for

[8] That is, it excludes bequests transmitted through educational expenditures of parents, acculturation in the home, and so on.

[9] See "Raising Incomes Through Manpower Training Programs," p. 91.

tuition and stipends while attending public *or* private trade schools or training centers.[10] An increased expectation of a bonus-job in the future should heighten the motivation of low productivity workers to undertake general training.

Subversion of the Minimum Wage Laws

Admitting the redundancy of continuing to flog a favorite whipping boy of economists, if we really want youngsters, women, and disadvantaged workers in general to work more, the minimum wage laws are the height of folly. The establishment of income maintenance and training subsidies should destroy much of the force of the purported egalitarian arguments for minimum wage laws. Training subsidies in fact constitute one way to subvert the minimum wage laws.

A Program of Graduated Migration Supplements

A program of graduated migration supplements is designed primarily to increase social stability by reducing massive and growing concentrations of the disadvantaged in large cities, to reduce the anxieties allegedly occasioned by long-distance moves of displaced workers and their families, and, perhaps,[11] to reduce the costs associated with the growth of a megalopolis. What is envisioned is a system of public relocation assistance grants to households in which the magnitude of the grant would be pegged to the following:

1. The intensity of distress at the origin, be it urban slum or rural backwater.
2. The growth potential of the place of destination.
3. The initial income of the household.
4. And, of course, the distance of the move and the size of the household.

Such a system is intended to induce socially desirable migratory streams. The benefits to any particular household would

[10] This system seems to have worked well enough under the post-World War II G.I. Bill. Are the current target groups really so different from veterans?

[11] The evidence that there is in fact an association between increases in urban scale and high per capita costs of public services is not very convincing, one way or the other.

depend both on its "need" and on the degree to which its actions accord with the fulfillment of social objectives.

A Program of Individual Tuition Assistance for All Levels of Education

The idea of a program of individual tuition assistance for all levels of education is hardly novel.[12] It is surprising, nevertheless, how much support it has been generating recently at both ends of the political spectrum. An appealing variant of it would simply issue vouchers to parents which could be used to pay educational costs for their children in schools of their own choosing. Some minimum public certification of schools would probably be required.

Current controversies over school decentralization would be defused: freedom of choice for parents is the ultimate in decentralization. All schools would be forced to compete for patronage rather than relying on captive markets, and their offerings would thus be upgraded. Compulsary attendance up to a certain age would continue. Students from poor families could be provided larger vouchers to bring about more ultimate equality of opportunity (especially since the more affluent would tend to supplement tuition payments out of their own funds). Certification need not be limited to schools operated by nonprofit groups. It has been argued, for example, that currently some of the best elementary and trade schools are operated for profit. In general, the more competition, the better. Tuition grants could be adjusted to encourage both whites and blacks to attend integrated schools.

A Significant Expansion of Rent Supplements

Adoption of the program recommended above would in time bring about the desired income distribution. There might still, however, be some reasons to encourage certain types of housing consumption for some groups. Let us assume there are. Then rent supplements for the low income, combined, perhaps, with house purchase down payment or interest supplements, would offer the following advantages over current housing programs:

[12] See, for example, Milton Friedman, James Coleman, Irving Kristol, Kenneth Clark, ond others.

1. Less "institutionalization" of the poor.
2. More integration.[13]
3. More incentive for research and technological change in low-cost residential construction.
4. More freedom of choice for beneficiaries in style, location, and so on.
5. Improved employment prospects for non-whites, to the extent that residential sites with better job access are chosen.[14]

A System of Housing Integration Bonuses

Suppose that each time a household changed the location of its residence it was determined whether their departure from their original census tract (*A*) would have the effect of bringing the minority group residence proportion in that census tract closer to the average for the metropolitan area within which tract *A* lies. Let it also be determined whether their settling in tract *B* would have the effect of bringing *B's* proportion closer to the metropolitan average. If the answer to both questions is yes, the household gets a public subsidy of *x* percent on the market rental or purchase price it will pay for the new dwelling unit and so does the landlord or seller of the dwelling unit to which it moves. This scheme[15] imposes a cost (sacrifice) directly on those with prejudice and/or compensates them for losses resulting from the prejudice of others (for example, other tenants, neighbors, and so on.)

Summary

I should like to reiterate the advantages of these kinds of programs. They are realistic in that they provide dollar re-

[13] Integration per se clearly is not as widely agreed upon an objective as we used to think. Still perhaps it is derivable from such stated objectives as equality of opportunity, liberty, and social stability.

[14] On the face of it, this idea is much superior to bribing firms to locate in ghettos, as has been proposed to accomplish the same end.

[15] The conception and development of this scheme are entirely attributable to I. S. Lowry. See Pascal, ed., *Cities in Trouble: An Agenda for Urban Research,* RM-5603-RC (Santa Monica: The Rand Corporation, 1968), pp. 24–25.

wards fairly directly in exchange for socially desirable results or actions (for example, education, work, integration). This also makes them relatively efficient. They are rather automatic and require less bureaucratic meddling and permit more freedom among program beneficiaries than the schemes they would replace.

All of them would seem to constitute attractive candidates for experiments and pilot programs.[16] Proper design and careful monitoring would permit the evaluations necessary before serious, broad-scale implementation.

Many significant social problems are not directly confronted by this list of proposed programs. Nothing is promised about ending race and class prejudice, increasing the dignity of the disadvantaged, enhancing the political and social power of minorities, or improving the quality of life in the United States. Though I agree that these are important goals, I will blame the social bias and moral naïveté of my profession for leading me to believe that such goals are almost necessarily beyond the reach of politics. And it is politics, after all, that program design and establishment are all about.

Are any of these ideas politically feasible? I can see no reason they should not be preferred to current programs by potential beneficiaries. The lineup of producer interest opponents, however, is likely to be rather impressive and include social workers, school teachers, labor unions, "neighborhood protective associations," and rural and slum congressmen, but not necessarily taxpayers, if the latter can be educated to the advantages of direct attacks on problems. As potential producer-interest allies I would suggest, however, computer manufacturers, home builders, private school entrepreneurs, business firms in general, and social scientists seeking contracts for program evaluation.

[16] For income maintenance and rent supplements, demonstrations are already in the works.

Raising Incomes Through Manpower Training Programs

Lester C. Thurow

Massachusetts Institute of Technology

The general tone of the following paper makes successful manpower training programs seem impossible, and perhaps they are.[1] All of the following ingredients are necessary: (1) an active program of adult remedial education to raise literacy levels to the point where on-the-job training can be effective; (2) a strong program of financial incentives for on-the-job training; (3) a government that is not only going to enforce existing fair employment laws but is going to use government contracts very aggressively to *demand* Negro employment; (4) a very tight labor market (3 percent unemployment) where desired increases in production must be curtailed if Negroes are not hired; (5) centralized administration of existing training programs at the local level with local freedom to innovate coupled with an active system of rewards and punishment for the administrator; and (6) aid to the employer to help him handle a different type of employee. The complementarities

[1] This paper is based on a joint discussion paper written with Mike Piore and David Taylor of the Massachusetts Institute of Technology. The conclusions, interpretations, and any errors are mine.

For a general discussion of manpower programs and a large collection of manpower statistics, see the annual *Manpower Reports of the President,* U.S. Department of Labor.

among these ingredients are large. One missing ingredient can make the others seem worthless.

I do not have any easy solutions. Success requires the elimination of discrimination and the past manifestations of discrimination. If the government does not take an active lead in cleaning up its own house (a major job in itself) and is not willing to use both the stick and the carrot on the private sector, no major breakthroughs can be seen on the employment front.

Background

Federal manpower training programs began before the current interest in antipoverty programs. They were originally designed to lower unemployment in the late 1950s and the early 1960s by eliminating structural unemployment. As aggregate demand lowered unemployment and the structural hypothesis became less tenable as an explanation of high unemployment, the manpower training programs gradually shifted character and became antipoverty programs rather than methods for solving the unemployment problem.[2]

They readily harmonized with the early puritan ethic of the war on poverty. Poverty was to be eliminated by raising everyone's marginal product to the level where he would be able to earn an acceptable income. Education and training programs were to be the principal means for raising marginal products. Although early poverty programs were based on the assumption that increasing workers' human capital could eliminate poverty, later and more sober analysis indicated that a major proportion of the poverty problem could not be solved by human capital programs. Large numbers of people were simply outside the productive labor force and could be brought into the productive labor force only at prohibitive costs. Analytically it is now generally realized that some large program of income redistribution will be necessary to eliminate poverty in anything but the very long run, but the political realization has yet to occur.[3]

[2] The specific uses of the approximately $2 billion in federal training funds can be found in the 1968 budget.

[3] Over 55 percent of poverty household heads were not at work or were over 65 years of age in 1965.

Federal antipoverty programs are still very much concentrated in the manpower training area. They can be divided into two distinct classes. (1) Some programs, such as the Manpower Development and Training Act (MDTA), are designed solely to equip individuals with skills that will increase their incomes. (2) Other programs, such as the Neighborhood Youth Corps and the Job Corps, use training as an incentive device to accomplish a host of social objectives. These programs are designed to provide incentives for further formal education, to improve health, to provide an integrated experience, to alter radically the individual's cultural and physical environment, to reduce juvenile delinquency, and to accomplish many other social objectives in addition to raising income levels.

The first class of institutional training programs should not be expanded and probably should be reduced in size. As an experiment they were justified, but they did not prove to be very successful. Cost-benefit results were mixed, but the costs per dollar of extra income provided were generally very high. The failures of institutional training programs of the first type are manifold. Programs did not provide workers with the salable skills demanded by industry. Union restrictions, the high specific training component of most jobs, and the general quality of training received meant that the individuals received training that did not have a marked effect on their income streams. (The programs suffered from the same problems that have plagued vocational education generally.) Since salable skills were not provided, there were no incentives to complete training courses. The low probability of finding a job at the end of a training program meant that the rational individual would drop out of the programs whenever a job became available rather than wait for a job for which he was being trained. The basic lack of jobs and the corresponding effects on incentives meant that the costs per dollar of additional income generated were very high. In addition, on-the-job training programs, despite their many faults, dominate institutional training programs of the first type. Their costs per dollar of income generated are much lower, though they still may be high. Even if this statement were not true, institutional training programs simply cannot be expanded fast enough to make a major reduction in the poverty problem. Governments do not have the personnel to operate programs of the necessary size.

If the second class of institutional training program is evaluated in the same manner as the first, a similar set of mixed results will be obtained.[4] The costs per additional dollar of income generated are high; but these programs do not solely aim, or even primarily aim, to raise income levels. The benefits are very diverse and are not limited to the extra dollars of income generated by the extra skills imparted by the programs. On-the-job training (OJT) programs do not dominate the second class of training programs for young persons because OJT cannot accomplish many of the objectives of these programs. Given the diverse social objectives of these programs, the verdict on their desirability is still out. They may or may not provide the desired social benefits. Probably the social objectives of these programs should be more explicitly recognized, but this would not necessarily mean a downgrading of the present training component of these programs. Training is absolutely essential to provide incentives to enter the programs, but it should be recognized that the training probably cannot justify itself in a narrow income-generated, cost-benefit framework.

Thus, institutional training for young people should be continued, but justified much more on a social benefit basis than on the present economic basis. Expanded institutional training for adults should be limited to remedial education programs designed to raise the level of literacy of an individual so that he can successfully participate in OJT programs. Because of the large complementarities between basic education and OJT programs, training programs cannot be successful unless individuals meet basic minimum standards of literacy.[5] Large-scale adult education programs should be designed to bring heads of families and other workers up to at least eighth and perhaps tenth grade standards of literacy. Unfortunately, the educational establishment is not interested in large-scale remedial adult education. Better education for the young is necessary, but it will not have any short-run effect on the poverty problem.[6]

[4] Glen Cain has an OEO cost-benefit analysis of the Job Corps which states that the Job Corps economically pays for itself at present cost levels.

[5] "The Occupational Distribution of the Returns to Education and Experience for Whites and Negroes," in the *JEC Compendium on Human Resources* and the *1967 Proceedings of the American Statistical Association.*

[6] Fourteen percent of family heads in 1965 had less than 8 years of

To be successful, remedial education programs will have to be explicitly linked to an OJT program. Without this connection individuals will not have sufficient incentives to complete the remedial education programs. Thus, certain standards of literacy should be demanded as a condition of entry into OJT. The government should provide the resources to guarantee that any individual will be trained to meet the literacy standards and give an absolute guarantee that a job with upgrading possibilities will be available upon reaching defined literacy standards.

Financial Incentives for On-the-Job Training

To make a substantial impact on poverty, financial incentives must be designed for private OJT programs. The real costs of training the hard-core unemployed or subemployed are high enough so that private firms simply will not (and should not be asked to) undertake any more than token training without financial incentives. What kind of financial incentives should be provided?

Both the present program of grants for OJT and institutional training suffer from a lack of ability to generalize. Governments do not possess the human resources necessary to expand programs to a size where they might have a measurable impact on poverty. Skilled teachers and adequate facilities are the bottlenecks for institutional training, and the impossibility of negotiating detailed contracts with every firm is the bottleneck for OJT. The basic manpower training need at the moment is a single generalizable incentive system to encourage private manpower training. Only the private economy has the capability of undertaking training programs of the desired magnitude.

Generalizable programs must turn toward general grant or tax incentives. This could be done by a general wage subsidy or by grants and tax credits to pay for some percentage of training costs. Wage subsidies are an inefficient means of gaining OJT unless they are made conditional upon providing training.

education, and 31 percent had less than 9 years of education. If functional literacy standards rather than formal schooling were considered, the number would be even larger.

If they are conditional on training, the subsidy might as well be given directly to training rather than indirectly through wages, a practice probably more acceptable to both labor and management.

Both general grants and tax credits for training suffer from some severe disadvantages. (1) They both encourage cost-plus training programs. Industry has very little incentive to economize. (2) They both require an enforcement mechanism: either the Department of Labor or the Internal Revenue Service would have to check on the costs and quality of training. Because most OJT is very informal, enforcement would present great difficulties. Many production costs could easily be made to look like training costs. Thus, the government would still be stuck in the middle of a firm's training problems. Despite their generalizable appearance, the programs might do little to minimize the need for government manpower to efficiently manage the programs. (3) Both programs potentially could involve a lot of dead weight loss. The government would be paying for many people who would have received training anyway. There is no method for completely eliminating this problem, but it can be minimized by restricting the grants or credits to those that meet poverty criteria. Yet here again enforcement would be necessary. OEO is currently thinking about an insurance system where private industry would be insured against the extra turnover costs of trying to train low-income workers. Such a system would have all the disadvantages of wage and training subsidies and would assume that the only source of higher training costs for low-income workers is their higher probability of leaving before training costs can be recovered. An alternative is to set up a corporate profit tax surcharge which is placed in a trust fund to be returned to industry for training purposes. Proceeds from this "benefit tax" could be used for the groups now being trained. (4) The tax credit scheme also introduces additional distortions into the tax system. The accompanying inefficiencies are debatable given all of the other distortions in the tax system, but the costs of additional inefficiencies in the tax system cannot be completely ignored.

Many but not all of the previous objections could be eliminated by a system of grants or tax credits for raising the income level of a person in poverty. Instead of providing payments for training programs, the firm is given a bonus depending on how much it is able to raise the income of a worker. Raising income levels from $1,000 to $5,000 over a five-year period might be worth a bonus of $3,000, or any other amount. Such bonus payments would not have the cost-plus nature of training grants and would provide incentives for new and cheaper training methods. If incomes could be raised without training programs, so much the better. The bonus would then be paid to eliminate some imperfection in the market and would be doubly justifiable.

Enforcement personnel would be necessary only to determine income levels at either end of the period and during the period if the bonus were spread out over time. They could do so easily using existing Internal Revenue records and would require only a file check by the computer. The government would not have to determine either the costs or quality of a training program and would not have to be involved with designing good training programs.

The dead weight loss problem could be minimized by limiting the bonus to poverty workers and by scaling the bonus down as higher income levels are reached. Thus, raising income levels from $0 to $2,000 is worth much more than raising income levels from $2,000 to $4,000. In fact, the program might well be opened to everyone with incomes under $5,000 per year, but with very small bonuses paid for income rises above the $3,500 level. The system has the advantage of encouraging both employment of new workers and upgrading of those already employed. To implement such a program, a rough idea of the extra costs of training hard-core poverty workers would need to be obtained.

Necessary Conditions for Successful Training Programs

Aggregate Policies

The need for minimum standards of basic literacy has already been mentioned, but there are other necessary conditions for successful manpower programs. Utilization rates in the labor force must be kept at very high levels. Negroes will be hired and upgraded only if there are no other potential sources of manpower. Trainees will acquire jobs only if there are shortages of trained individuals. High utilization rates do not solve Negro and poverty employment problems, but they have large direct effects and even larger indirect effects through their complementarities with other programs. Tight labor markets are especially important to the problem of upgrading minority groups after they have jobs. If the inflation at a 3 percent unemployment rate is intolerable, then Negro employment gains will not be made.

Existing Federal Programs

Certain of the federal programs have been destructive of a viable long-run solution. This is particularly true of the temporary efforts to buy off discontent in the ghetto. Such programs have been designed to get large numbers of people off the street and to put money into their hands. The jobs offered have been either make work or menial. Such jobs increase the distaste and disrespect for work among the hard core, and hence they aggravate attitudes that already constitute a major bar to secure, high-paying jobs. Where employers have participated, the experience with the program has reinforced their initial prejudice against hard-core groups. Ideally, programs of this kind should be eliminated. If it is deemed necessary to disguise income transfers by tying them to work projects, the projects should be isolated as much as possible from other manpower programs.

The major contribution of federal manpower efforts has been the development of a group of people skilled in the techniques of adjusting the hard core to high-paying jobs. If existing programs were disbanded, these people would be scattered to other employments, and their skills lost to society. Since very little of what has been learned about adjustment techniques is recorded, the experience of the last two years would be lost with these people as well. Any solution to the problem, whether carried out by the government or by private employers, will require these techniques; and the desirability of preserving what has already been learned constitutes the major reason for preserving the federal programs.

It must be noted, however, that almost all of the skills and knowledge developed in existing programs are quite specific.

They involve, for example, such things as how to teach adult literacy effectively, how to recruit in the ghetto, how to train line supervision to manage the ghetto workers, and how to overcome problems of punctuality and attendance. The problem of teaching line management to handle ghetto workers is especially important. Foremen are generally untrained in the problems they face with hard-core poverty workers. They are usually unsympathetic to the problems of Negroes since they come from ethnic backgrounds that feel most threatened by Negroes.

We know almost nothing about the relative effectiveness of money spent on work orientation versus skill training, for example; or recruitment versus transportation; or training workers to respond to supervision versus the training of existing supervision to manage the workers. Nor do we know how various different approaches interrelate with each other. We do not know, for example, whether a preceding work orientation program increases the effectiveness of skill training. The data that would permit such judgments have not been collected; for most programs it is too late to collect such information.

The reason the data have not been collected is that, as the programs are administered at the present time, there is no incentive to do so. Funds have been allocated for specific programs (for example, Neighborhood Youth Corps, Work Experience and Training Program, MDTA); local administrators are assigned to the programs and carry them out. Washington gives them neither time nor money to evaluate what they are doing. How Washington makes a judgment is unclear.

To make effective use of existing institutional manpower programs, they must be centralized under a local administrator who has the power to alter programs and to innovate. The local administrator should then have an explicit benefit index to use in judging his work. Perhaps the index could be:

$$I = \frac{\sum_{i=1}^{w} w_i \Delta Y_i}{C}$$

where ΔY_i = change in income of the ith individual
w = income weight for the ith individual based on his initial income. The weight would go down as initial income goes up
C = program costs

Alternative indices could be suggested, but some simple way needs to be devised to focus administrative attention on the real goals of training programs while leaving the local administration free to adjust to local problems.

Management Reactions

Initial experience with hard-core employees tends to reinforce employers' prejudices against ghetto workers. Any plant must make certain accommodations when it introduces previously excluded groups of workers. If it does not make these accommodations, it will inevitably incur additional costs. Employers who have voluntarily hired hard-core workers have felt no necessity of thinking about accommodations, let alone making them, and they have tended to meet the problems they encountered by reversing the new policy. They are unlikely to begin making the required accommodations unless forced to do so. There is a strong analogy here to the impact of union organization: whatever the expense of union organization, it is considerably less if management revises its policies to accommodate the union. American management did not, on the whole, make this accommodation until forced to do so by the Wagner Act, and the pre-Wagner Act experience with trade unions acted to strengthen management resistance to them. The change in managerial policy we ought to be requiring at this juncture is no less (but also no more) than that required by the Wagner Act. The relationships between management hiring standards and job performance also needs to be investigated to see which standards are relevant to employee selection.

Direct Programs to Eliminate Discrimination

The federal government has three instruments for attacking discrimination in employment. Direct measures can be taken to end discrimination in government employment, the Office of Contract Compliance (OFCC) can be used to end discrimination in firms where the federal government makes purchases, and the Equal Employment Opportunity Commission (EEOC) can be used to end discrimination in general private employment. None of the three direct measures have been used very effectively.

The EEOC has no enforcement powers and can only investigate. Cases do not have to be taken seriously until they reach court and here they can be delayed almost indefinitely. OFCC has the statutory power to cut off contracts, a power that places it at odds with the contracting agency, usually the Defense Department, and OFCC seldom wins in the showdown. Efforts to eliminate discrimination in federal employment have been very mixed.[7] In strong, independent agencies with southern support, such as the Department of Agriculture, little progress has been made. The federal government remains an employer with some of the most restrictive hiring practices in the country. Civil Service Examinations are not closely related to job performances. Prison records are a bar to federal employment.

If the federal government is to eliminate hiring discrimination, it will need to make the following changes:

(1) Permit the OFCC to impose heavy fines upon employers who are not in compliance. They should be large enough to jeopardize the profitability of a contract.

(2) Give the EEOC the power to issue cease and desist orders enforceable in federal courts.

(3) Shift the burden of proof in both EEOC and OFCC complaints from the complainant, where it now seems to rest, to the plaintiff.

(4) Specifically outlaw hiring and promotion criteria which cannot be shown to be causally linked to job performance on the job for which the applicant is hired.

(5) Government contracts should be let with a clause specifying that after the date the contract goes into effect, some fairly large percentage of all new hires must be selected from low-income groups or poverty area residents. These individuals must be trained for regular jobs, but the costs of doing so can be included in the contract bid.

(6) Minority group hiring quotas should be placed on all government agencies.

[7] See Samuel Krislov, *The Negro in Federal Employment: The Quest for Equal Opportunity* (Minneapolis: University of Minnesota Press, 1967).

Summary

There is no doubt that such a set of programs would be unpopular in many (and perhaps most) quarters, but strong actions of this magnitude are necessary to make substantial progress in minority group employment. If they are politically impossible, large minority group employment gains are politically impossible.

Fewer Births—More Welfare

Stephen Enke

General Electric–TEMPO

Summary

The United States government's official policy is to make almost all forms of birth control available through federally supported programs to those, primarily the poor, who ask for information and means. Implementation of this policy has been slow and weak, although in 1967 Congress significantly increased fiscal year (FY) 1968 funding for birth control. Of the 5 million women who are believed to need and want assisted planned parenthood, about 0.7 million (or 14 percent) receive it. Currently the initiative comes usually from local communities, with federal agencies playing a passive but decreasingly hesitant role.

The association between many children and family poverty, which is both a cause and an effect, is well established. Poorer families have more children. The child of a poor *large* family has about half the probability of completing high school that the child of a poor *small* family has. Infant mortality rates are higher and measured intelligence is lower among children of large families. Nonwhites typically have larger families than whites, regardless of income.

There is scattered evidence that poor families want fewer children than nonpoor families. Yet the poor have larger families. This apparent "performance failure" of the poor is the result of some uncertain combination of poverty, ignorance, isolation from clinics, carelessness, and weak or unsustained motivation.

Various cost-benefit analyses suggest that the dollar return to governments on planned parenthood expenditures, in terms of saved welfare benefits, ranges upward from a ratio of 25 to 1. It is widely believed among many social workers that public funds to assist poor families in limiting their progeny can, in the long run, be a more effective antipoverty measure than any other. For those poor families that otherwise would have an additional and unwanted child within a year, birth control assistance brings some relief within 12 months.

Areas urgently requiring study include: (1) What more exactly are the cause and effect relations between family size and income? (2) Why do some poor families use contraceptives while others do not? (3) What methods of contraception are most economical for which kinds of women and men under what circumstances? (4) What government-supported programs making voluntary birth control more available are likely to reduce poverty most for a given budget? (5) How can conceptually sound yet practicable cost-benefit ratios be determined?

Introduction

The first birthright of a child is to be wanted, and the unwanted child often fares less well in life. Preferences differ among parents of different income and culture, but most state a desire for two or three children. The number of North American parents who want more than three children is about half that who state a preference for three or fewer.[1]

The poor generally *want* fewer children than the nonpoor want, especially if they are urban residents; but they *have*

[1] Arthur A. Campbell, "The 'Growth of American Families' Studies," *Welfare in Review* (October, 1965).

larger families as much in cities as in the countryside. Surveys of parents having six or more children indicate that they wanted no more than four (that is, at least two fewer children) and that they were disproportionately among the poor.[2]

In North America, middle-class families, including many nominally Catholic families, do plan their families. On the whole they decide the date of first birth, subsequent spacing, and final family size. This is evidenced by the marked changes in age-specific birth rates that seem to follow fashion (for example, low birth rates in the 1930s and larger families in the late 1950s).

Poor families, however, and especially those from disadvantaged minorities (Negroes, Puerto Ricans, and Mexicans), are not in control to the same extent. Often they are unaware of the very idea of planned parenthood, ignorant of methods now existing, uncertain where to go for advice and help, afraid of expense, too resigned to take the necessary first step, and sometimes too weak-minded or forgetful to use the means provided them. Some of the poor do not have the sustained motivation and necessary dependability to practice birth control.

The majority of poor parents, who typically have families of above average size, fortunately could use modern control techniques however. Use of an intrauterine device (IUD) requires one decisive act; once inserted, the IUD functions "automatically" if retained. For most poor families the problem is that they do not know where to go, or whom to ask for what.

The trouble is not merely that our governments have taken such limited and hesitating steps in the direction of assisting the poor to help themselves by limiting their numbers of children. Even when government support exists, it too often remains unknown to those for whom it is intended. Necessary and overdue are more clinics, located in city areas where the poor live, and informational advertising through spot radio announcements (including "spots" on Spanish language stations where there are Puerto Rican and Mexican populations.)[3]

[2] *Ibid.;* also Elinor Langer, "Birth Control: U.S. Programs Off to Slow Start," *Science* (May 12, 1967); and *Studies in Family Planning* (New York: The Population Council).

[3] In this section particularly, a "poor" family is one which spends less than 70 cents per day per family member on food.

Association Between Family Size and Poverty

Poor parents have more children.[4] Children of large poor families are less likely to escape poverty through education and other means than children of small poor families. There is a vicious circle that apparently can be broken in many instances through effective birth control.

Table 1 shows that larger families are disproportinately likely to be poorer families, based on U.S. Census returns.

Table 2 shows that the dependency ratio (that is, the number of children under 18 in families per 100 persons in the prime working ages) is almost twice as great among the poor as among the nonpoor. It is especially high among nonwhites.

TABLE 1 Distribution of Poor and Nonpoor Children by Family Size

	Poor families	Nonpoor families
All families with children (percent)	*100*	*100*
1 to 2 children (percent)	43	64
3 to 4 children (percent)	34	29
5 or more children (percent)	23	7
Number of families (in thousands)	4,319	28,550
Number of children (in thousands)	13,937	55,692
Mean number of children per family	3.23	2.30

Studies in Family Planning, The Population Council, New York, p. 2.

TABLE 2 Dependency Ratios of the Poor and Nonpoor (Whites and Nonwhites), 1966

	Poor			Nonpoor		
	All	White	Nonwhite	All	White	Nonwhite
Number of children under 22 per 100 persons aged 22 to 64	148	128	197	79	78	88

[4] Frederick S. Jaffe, *Closing the Gap in Subsidized Family Planning Services in 110 Metropolitan Areas With More than 250,000 Population* (Planned Parenthood—World Population, October, 1967).

Over half of all nonwhite children are members of poor families.

There are indications that children of poor families are more likely to escape poverty if they are members of small rather than large families. Additional education is recognized as one means of gaining a higher income. An analysis of 45 million adult men shows that 73 percent of those with no siblings, 60 percent of those with one to three siblings, and 39 percent of those with four or more completed high school.[5]

Children from small families tend to make higher scores on intelligence tests, perhaps because they are more in contact with adults. And children from small families are more likely to rise above their father's status than those of large families. There are also two conclusions of a stratified sample study of all children born in England and Wales in one week of March, 1946.[6]

The qualitative linkages (inverse) between family size and income can be postulated more easily than proved. The mother of many children has fewer years in which she can work gainfully outside the home. Her health is often affected so that some older child, usually a daughter, must stay home more to look after the younger children. Often each child gets less food, not enough protein and vitamins, and suffers retarded growth. The need to earn income sooner may preclude the child's continuing his education. Less education and poor health tend to be reflected in lower income in later years because the family head is less able to save against emergencies.

The Existing Gap

The "gap" between the number of indigents supposedly wanting family planning assistance and those currently receiving it appears very wide. In the 110 standard metropolitan areas (SMAs), which contain 306 counties, it is estimated that there are 2.7 million poor women in need of subsidized family

[5] Peter M. Blau and Otis Dudley Duncan, *The American Occupational Structure* (New York: John Wiley & Sons, 1967).

[6] John Nisbet, in A. H. Halsey (ed.), *Education, Economy, and Society* (New York: Free Press, 1961), pp. 273–287. Also, Dr. John Clausen, in Lois and Martin Hoffman (eds.), *Review of Child Development Research* (New York: Russell Sage Foundation, 1966), pp. 12–14.

planning services. Of these, 452,000, or 17 percent, were apparently receiving such help in 1967 from the following agencies: health department clinics, 127,000; public and voluntary hospitals, 177,000; Planned Parenthood Centers, 141,000; and other organized services, 7,000.

Thus about 2.25 million women, or 83 percent of those in need, remain unserved in the 110 largest metropolitan areas of the United States. At least 175 government health departments in these 110 areas provide no family planning assistance. In these same areas there are 764 non-Catholic hospitals providing no such services either. These same hospitals delivered a million babies in 1965, or over half the babies born in these areas. It may be that 75 percent of the babies born in the United States are born in hospitals providing no organized family planning assistance.

In New York City, it is estimated that 176,000 poor patients need family planning and are not now served, that is, 68 percent of the need is not being met. The total estimated need of 259,000 is believed to come 75 percent from white families and 25 percent from nonwhite. There are 54 non-Catholic hospitals delivering over 500 babies a year and 29 health department clinics offering no family planning assistance.

About 85 percent of all U.S. Community Action Programs (CAPs) against poverty in 1967 did not include family planning programs and support. The CAPs of New York, Chicago, and Los Angeles, for instance, did not include any. The largest city that did was St. Louis.[7]

Government Attitudes Toward Birth Control

The attitude of the federal government toward planned parenthood as a means of contributing to welfare has been characterized through 1966 at least as "leaderless and leisurely"[8] despite public support of family planning by the President. However, in December, 1967, Congress may have provided adequate funding for the immediate future.

In March, 1966, President Lyndon B. Johnson stated in a message to Congress, "It is essential that all families have

[7] Jaffe, *Closing the Gap* . . . .

[8] Mollie Orshansky, "Who's Who Among the Poor: A Demographic View of Poverty," *Social Security Bulletin* (July, 1965).

access to information and services that will allow freedom to choose the number and spacing of their children within the dictates of individual conscience." However, despite the fanfare, the new policy was hardly reflected in programs during 1967. A few hundred thousand women at most had so far been affected.

In late 1967 Congress passed two important amendments. An amendment to the Social Security Act provided that 6 percent of all federal appropriations for maternal and child care should hereafter be used to support family planning services (or about $15 million in FY 1968). An amendment to the Public Assistance Act requires states and their minor jurisdictions, as a condition of receiving federal aid, to provide family planning assistance "whenever appropriate." How the Department of Health, Education, and Welfare (DHEW) will interpret this mandate, and how it will be implemented by states, counties, and cities, has yet to be determined. Nevertheless, on the face of it, Congress may have established at least two important precedents in 1967.

The Department of Health, Education, and Welfare

It is difficult to isolate the exact amount DHEW-supported programs have recently been spending on birth control because the department does not support planned parenthood as such. It supports "comprehensive health service," as proposed by the states, which may include birth control assistance. This policy tends to shield DHEW from attack by those opposed to giving the poor the sort of contraceptive knowledge that nearly all nonpoor couples use. Altogether, DHEW-related programs for birth control assistance appear to have cost $3 million in 1966 and $9 million in 1967.

DHEW has established a new position of Deputy Assistant Secretary for Population and Science. The first incumbent had no supporting staff, and most of his time was spent on matters other than population.

The Office of Economic Opportunity

The OEO did not stride into the family-planning arena so much as it was pushed there through Community Action Programs. Initially there was a general reluctance in Washington to support local requests for birth control assistance because of largely unfounded fears of political objections based on religion. At the outset, there were many restrictions. For instance, these services were allowed only for married women, although a greater need exists among unmarried girls and abandoned women. OEO still will not fund vasectomies. OEO funds cannot be used to advertise the availability of family planning information. Until 1967 OEO had no special staff member for family planning.

OEO funding through CAP of family planning assistance has been $2.4 million in FY 1966 and $4.6 million in FY 1967.

In 1967 family planning assistance became yet another "national emphasis program"; however, there are seven national emphasis programs. Some, such as Head Start, have had a head start (compared with birth control programs) when it comes to funding.

The Bureaucratic Problem

All in all, the federal government spent about $35 million in 1967 to assist family planning (compared with $40 million for rat control.) How is it, despite recognition of the inverse relation between family size and income, that so little is being done? The cost-benefit ratio appears very high. President Johnson courageously proclaimed a policy of support. Most initial fears of political objections have largely been overcome. The problem lies in bureaucratic inertia. It takes a new official, with new interests and knowledge, to introduce new programs: a man identified with tuberculosis programs will not readily shift his energies to birth control programs. And in a period of tight budgets, new programs can be added only by subtracting old ones (usually difficult politically and administratively).

Cost-Benefit Considerations

There are many ways in which the cost-benefit relation of government spending to assist voluntary birth control, especially among poorer families, can be approached. In "micro" terms, there is the question of which methods are best for which people. A common and broader approach is to consider what governments may save over time in reduced welfare costs of all kinds as a result of fewer births, but this is not always logical because outlays for schooling, for example, may enable people to exit from poverty and increase their taxpaying ability. A really "macro" approach to estimating the cost-benefit relation is conceptually simple but practically very difficult. The best that can be done may be to reach judgments based on many partial (fragmentary) calculations.

Choice of Method

There are many methods of contraception, including withdrawal, rhythm, condoms, spermicides, caps, pills, intrauterine devices, and sterilization. They all involve some costs; even withdrawal and rhythm involve an initial educational cost to be reasonably effective. Pills have an almost zero initial cost but a relatively high monthly cost. Male and female sterilization have a once-for-all cost. Condoms involve a smaller or larger money outlay than pills depending upon frequency of intercourse. For prolonged contraception, over several years, an IUD insertion is cheaper than pills (the major cost of which is no longer production but distribution).

The effectiveness of these methods varies somewhat even when used by disciplined people with strong motivation. In practice, users vary in foresight, willpower, and memory. Pills provide questionable protection if not taken every day between menses. A man may have forgotten to supply himself with condoms. A girl may not have expected she would need her diaphragm. Thus the practical effectiveness of different methods varies enormously, as do their cost-benefit ratios.

Conceptually, it is possible to state the cost per birth prevented, given age-specific fertilities, for each alternative method. Which in cost-benefit terms is the "best" method depends on what the constraint is. If the constraint is available budget, an "inferior" biological method (for example, withdrawal) may prevent the most births if it is also very cheap per additional user. If the constraint is number of voluntary participants, some of the biologically more efficient methods that also cost more per user may be economically warranted. To what extent a government might prefer voluntary participants to shift to a biologically more effective and financially more costly method will depend on the value to government in some sense of extra birth preventions.[9]

Practically, a government must offer a wide variety of methods, and hope that the mix of methods used involves benefit-to-cost ratios equal to or greater than similar rates for rival human betterment programs.

Returns to Government

From the public viewpoint, as distinct from that of individual users, one can imagine the federal government (plus state and local governments, perhaps) estimating the return to the treasury on spending for birth control assistance in terms of future welfare savings (for example, reduction in payments and cost of services.)

Conceptually, each infant has a potential for costing government money during his subsequent life. His birth may cost government funds, his education does, and later he will receive various social services and payments. The same infant gives promise during his life of making payments to governments through taxes and the like.

Infants born into rich families, or infants who become rich, will pay more in taxes to government than they will ever receive from it in value of services or unearned money (neglecting defense services). Infants born into poor families may, during their lifetimes, receive more from government, measuring services and cash receipts in dollars, than they provide in taxes. And the fifth, sixth, and seventh children of poor families are apparently more likely to be mentally retarded, to have health problems, and to pay fewer taxes than the children of small families.

Imagining federal, state, and local governments as a collective profits maximizer, in terms of discounted or undiscounted cash flows, it appears most probable that the "last" children of large poor families occasion a "loss" to governments (and

[9] Stephen Enke, *Economic Programs to Prevent Births,* U.S., World Population Conference, Belgrade, September, 1965; and "The Economic Aspects of Slowing Population Growth," *The Economic Journal* (March, 1966).

hence taxpayers). Consider a simple "understating" example. A woman in her twenties, who has some dependent children and is receiving welfare payments about 30 weeks a year, has a fertility rate of perhaps 0.2 a year. If she has an extra child, government may pay her an extra $900 a year, so that the statistical or expected cost to government is $180 a year. The cost of having that woman practice birth control is, say, $18 a year. The return would be 10 to 1.

Planned Parenthood Federation estimates more carefully that each $10 million will fund an effective birth control program for one year in which 500,000 women participate (at $20 each annually). It has estimated that this will provide a saving of about $250 million in reduced expenditures for maternal and child health care, aid to dependent children, care of retardates, and so on. This 25-to-1 rate of return is almost certainly an understatement. It is based on an incomplete count of government welfare expenditures. Also the government cost items that are included, and some that were not but might have been, do not generally result in increased economic output by the beneficiaries. It is reported that unpublished DHEW staff studies show returns approaching 75 to 1.

This whole "return to government" approach suffers from obvious limitations. It attributes a distinct personality and motivation to "government." Some government welfare expenditures involve resource costs on the economy, such as child care centers. Others are transfer payments with little resource cost except for administration, such as relief. Welfare programs also are "good" or "bad" in many ways that are not exactly reflected in cash flows between beneficiaries and government.

An Overall Approach

There is a still more overall or "macro" approach to estimating the worth of birth control, more logical conceptually, but more difficult to undertake. It involves not merely considering what an extra child "does" to governments but what it "does" to the whole national economy (including all governments.)

The average person, during his or her life, produces marketed goods and services of greater value than the marketed goods and services he or she consumes. (The difference is national saving.) Men typically have a large "export" balance, women an "import" one, as services provided within the household and not marketed are not taken into account here. A child diverts consumption and savings from his parents and siblings, and an adult contributes to its own dependents. Also, as indicated above, each person has a payments balance with government units (taking costs of government services as a "payment" to the beneficiary.)

Children born into well-to-do homes tend to "give" more than they "receive," primarily because they will receive government services of modest cost (even going to private schools perhaps) and paying considerable taxes as adults (for the education and care of other families in part). Children born into small, poor families are more likely to climb the socioeconomic ladder than those born into large, poor families. They may take from their childhood family less than they give to the families they form. Once again, the target families of publicly assisted birth control should be poor families who already have three or more living children.

At least theoretically, there is some discount rate that renders the present value of all infants born this year to be zero. This discount rate should be in accord with the national rate of return on invested capital if the rate of natural increase, in terms of population/capital-to-labor-force ratios, is economically "correct." It follows that certain kind of infants, categorized in terms of the families they would be born into, will have negative values at birth. Such families should be given every opportunity to practice birth control. Governments can expend additional resources to provide them with the knowledge and means.

Although such a judgment is partly subjective, it is not a mystery as to which categories of families are most likely to have extra children that will drain more away from the economy than they can ever contribute. Large minority families, having low incomes, the parents suffering from poor health and education, are an obvious target group. And yet these families often seem least aware of family planning means.

Urgently Needed Research

Research on the physiology of human reproduction, as a means of both promoting and preventing it, will continue anyway. The white nonpoor, Catholic as well as Protestant, will continue to use one or other method of contraception. Not so certain are the answers to a number of questions fundamental to government support of voluntary birth control as an antipoverty measure.

What are the cause and effect relations between family size and income? The association between poverty and many children has been noted for centuries. Are the parents poor because they have many children? Why are the children of large families likely to become poor parents. Tentative conclusions exist, but more surveys and documentation could be important.

Why do some poor families use contraceptives while others do not? A little but not much is known of the specific obstacles preventing some families from using contraceptives. Sometimes it is simple ignorance of how babies are "made." Dependent children payments may temporarily encourage larger families among the poor. Some poor parents are unaware of the very concept of family planning. Others have no idea of where to go or whom to ask for assistance. Many lack the sustained motivation to make certain methods effective. A few lack the funds to buy the means. Until more surveys have been made, the best mix of assistance measures is hard to determine. For instance, how important is rescaling payments for dependent children, or having conveniently located clinics, or advertising where to go? Through pooled record-keeping, women who visit clinics could be tracked more systematically, to learn if their interest is sustained and how it accorded with performance.

What methods of contraception are most economical for which kinds of men and women? Any public birth control assistance program must probably offer all kinds of methods, including the rhythm method, regardless of practical effectiveness; but some are more economical than others, depending on such circumstances as frequency of intercourse, desire for extra children later but not now, attitudes of resident in-laws, dependability of the participating spouse, and so on. More needs to be known about effectiveness in practice and resource costs, irrespective of who nominally "pays."

What government-supported programs making voluntary birth control more available are likely to reduce poverty most for a given budget? From a budget, more or less can be spent on establishing neighborhood clinics, in explaining the idea of spacing and control, in advertising the existence of free assistance clinics, in staffing them with qualified doctors or nondoctors, in providing incentives to privately practicing doctors, in providing means at subsidized or zero prices, and so on. What is best will depend upon the cultural and other characteristics for the target population, but how is not yet well understood.

How can cost-benefit ratios be determined that are conceptually sound yet practicable too? Such cost benefit ratios are needed for logical government programming of birth control. In fact the economics profession has not yet provided them, partly because of a general lack of interest. But were it otherwise, the task would still be a difficult and challenging one.

Bibliography

Blau, Peter M. and Otis Dudley Duncan. *The American Occupational Structure,* New York: John Wiley & Sons, 1967.

Bogue, D. J., ed. *Sociological Contributions to Family Planning Research.* Chicago, 1967.

Calderone, Mary S. *Manual of Contraceptive Practice.* Baltimore: Williams & Wilkins Company, 1964.

Campbell, Arthur A. "The 'Growth of American Families' Studies," *Welfare in Review* (October, 1965).

——, "The Family Planning and the Reduction of Poverty in the United States," an unpublished report submitted to The Secretary's Task Force on Exits from Poverty, June, 1967.

Chilman, Catherine S. "Poverty and Family Planning in the U.S.," *Welfare in Review* (April, 1967).

——, "Population Dynamics and Poverty in the United States," *Welfare in Review* (June–July, 1966).

——, *Growing Up Poor,* DHEW, Welfare Administration Publication No. 13 (May, 1966).

Corkey, Elizabeth C. "A Family Planning Program for the Low-Income Family," *Journal of Marriage and Family* (November, 1964).

Enke, Stephen. *Economic Programs to Prevent Births,* U.S., World Population Conference, Belgrade, September, 1965.

——, "The Economic Aspects of Slowing Population Growth," *The Economic Journal* (March, 1966).

Freedman, Ronald and Lolagene Coombs. "Child Spacing and Family Economic Position," *American Sociological Review* (October, 1966).

Furie, Sidney. "Birth Control and the Lower Class Unmarried Mother," *Social Work* (January, 1966).

Gans, H. "Poverty and Culture: Some Basic Questions About Methods of Studying Life-Styles of the Poor," prepared for the International Seminar on Poverty, University of Essex, April, 1967.

Halsey, A. H., ed. *Education, Economy, and Society.* New York: Free Press, 1961.

Harkavy, Oscar, Frederick S. Jaffe, and Samuel M. Wishik. *Implementing DHEW Policy on Family Planning and Population: A Consultants' Report.* September, 1967. Mimeographed.

Hoffman, Lois, and Martin Hoffman, eds. *Review of Child Development Research.* New York: Russell Sage Foundation, 1966.

Hill, Adelaide Cromwell and Frederick S. Jaffe. "Negro Fertility and Family Size Preferences," in *The Negro American.* Boston: Houghton Mifflin, 1966.

Hill, R., J. M. Stycos, and K. W. Back. *The Family and Population Control.* Chapel Hill: University of North Carolina Press, 1959.

Jaffe, Frederick S. *Closing the Gap in Subsidized Family Planning Services in 110 Metropolitan Areas with More Than 250,000 Population.* Planned Parenthood—World Population, October, 1967.

———, *Family Planning and Rural Poverty: An Approach to Programming of Services.* Prepared for the National Advisory Commission on Rural Poverty, June, 1967.

Langer, Elinor. "Birth Control: U.S. Programs Off to Slow Start," *Science* (May 12, 1967).

Orshansky, Mollie. "Who's Who Among the Poor: A Demographic View of Poverty," *Social Security Bulletin* (July, 1965).

Sheppard, Harold L. *The Effects of Family Planning on Poverty in the United States,* Kalamazoo, Michigan: W. E. Upjohn Institute for Employment Research, October, 1967.

Studies in Family Planning. New York: The Population Council.

Whelpton, Pascal K., Arthur A. Campbell, and John E. Patterson, *Fertility and Family Planning in the U.S.* Princeton: University Press, 1966.

Welfare—Problems and Research

Nathan Glazer

Harvard University

Welfare in this country is something like public housing. We have a system that in its broad essentials was set up in the middle 1930s and was viewed then as a triumph of liberal and progressive principles. Twenty years later the same progressives and liberals, or their descendants, consider these programs niggardly, punitive, and overly restrictive. Beyond that, they argue that these programs are, in some respects, responsible for the continuation of the conditions they were meant to overcome (dependency, poor housing); finally, and most recently, the antagonism to these programs has become even more extreme, and they are attacked as being not only insufficient and counterproductive, but also, in some measure, unconstitutional in their regulations and restrictions. The two programs share something else in common: the same solutions have been again and again proposed to remedy their defects. These solutions seem more impressive to the critics than to the administrators of the programs; and even when they finally come into effect, it turns out that the administrators have had some justice on their side, that is, that there are indeed no simple solutions.

Three points have been commonly made in discussion of welfare, its inadequacies, and how they might be remedied:

more money, more case work, and more power to welfare recipients. These are discussed in the sections that follow.

More Money

One popular point of view on welfare is that the burden of welfare is quite small for a rich country, that it is not that much of a problem, and we could easily increase the sums required to provide a decent minimal income for all persons on welfare. If we place total welfare costs in the context of the national budget or gross national product (GNP), they are not large. In recent years welfare payments in the federal budget have been about $3 billion; in addition, we now spend over $1 billion for medical assistance for the medically indigent, including those on welfare. This is about 3 or 4 percent of the budget. The welfare burden is heavier for the states, which cannot increase their revenues so easily. And it is also heavy for localities. New York City, which appropriated $950,000,000 out of a budget of more than $5 billion in 1966–67, got $363 million from the federal government and $288 million from the state, but had to raise $267 million—no minor sum—in local taxes. Actually the burdens are heaviest in the most generous states, such as New York, California, and Illinois. (The most recent year for which I have overall national figures, 1965, shows a $2.9 billion federal expenditure for welfare, $1.8 billion from states, and $.6 billion from local governments. New York City supplies something like one-third of all the *local* funds spent on welfare in the United States!) Although it is true the burden of welfare is not heavy, it *is* heavy for those states and those cities most adequately and most generously supporting the welfare population. At the best support levels, welfare costs do become a serious burden.

But even assuming the burden in those states that are most generous is not too severe, and could be increased somewhat to satisfy the critics of welfare, would that contribute to the solution of the welfare problem? Is the problem of welfare in short that we are too niggardly in supporting the poor? For some of the major categories of the poor, this is indeed the problem—for the aged, the blind, and the disabled. There we do not expect any work contribution; work for these categories is seen more as a form of therapy than as a contribution to the national welfare. For these categories there could be no argument against a fairly generous allowance. Most of these allowances are too low and should be raised.

Different problems arise, however, for the largest and most rapidly growing component of the welfare population, those who come under Aid to Families with Dependent Children (AFDC). These are families who do not have a wage-earner as a head, and who have children under 18. The great majority are headed by women who are widows, or whose husbands have abandoned them, or who have illegitimate children and have never had husbands. Initially, this part of the welfare program was considered as largely temporary, just as Old Age Assistance (OAA) was once considered temporary, because as more and more of the population earned full coverage under Social Security, they would be supported in old age by Social Security; and if they died and left young children, their widows and children would be covered by survivor's insurance. This expectation has been fulfilled by the aged, whose numbers on OAA have dropped steadily since 1950, but not by AFDC recipients. After dropping in number in the early 1950s, they have been rising steadily in number since, and the rise has been most steep in recent years. In October, 1967, 5.1 million of those on welfare were on AFDC, as against 2.1 million on OAA, 7 million on Aid to the Disabled and Aid to the Blind, and 0.7 million on General Assistance. In that month, even though Social Security had been in effect for about 30 years, the children supported under Old-Age, Survivors, and Disability Insurance was 2.8 million, as against a larger number of 3.9 million under AFDC. It is somewhat startling to see how many children had never been covered by a wage earner under Social Security.

No serious problem is raised when we consider solving the welfare problems of the aged, blind, and disabled; the answer is money and consideration, and these categories need more. In England, for example, there is now a program to provide specially equipped cars to the disabled; we should be thinking of the same kind of imaginative assistance.

Three problems stand in the way of generous support as the full solution. First, the question does come up, perhaps more of the mothers should work. This is the main thrust of the new welfare amendments Congress has just passed, freezing AFDC payments to the proportion of children under 18 in each state who are receiving AFDC on January 1, 1968, and providing day care for children so mothers will be encouraged to work. If work is good for some of the mothers, and perhaps even good for the children because they will have happier mothers, how do we maintain incentives to work at generous levels of support? Second, a more emotion-laden question arises, and that is that a substantial proportion of the children on AFDC are illegitimate, and legislatures are torn between the social worker's plea to provide generous support and their antagonism to mothers on welfare who have illegitimate children. Is there an incentive to have more children? Certainly conservative legislators think so. The idea that mothers should work, or that mothers should not have illegitimate children might be problems only for conservatives and reactionaries, but hovering above these objections to generous support to mothers with dependent children as a full solution to their problem is the widespread belief that welfare degrades people and makes them dependent, rather than restoring them to a self-respecting and dignified independence. This point of view is held by left as well as right. The average welfare check for AFDC in New York City for a mother and two children is $63.80 a week. (It is not much less in the better-off industrial states, somewhat less in other northern states, and very much less in the South.) Would their lives be very different at $100 a week? Yes for them (a good-enough reason); but would we consider that we had solved our welfare problems if the average support went up 50 percent or 100 percent? I don't think so.

To sum up the problems that bother us even when support is adequate:

1. The mothers should be encouraged to get off welfare; in other words, welfare is dependency. This argument is more popular with the right than the left, but sometimes we hear something of this kind from the left: welfare breeds dependency. I wonder how legitimate a problem this is? Do we *want* mothers of children under 18 to work?

2. The mothers are degraded by the requirements involved in meeting welfare. In most cities and states one of the chief problems is that the family is not eligible for welfare if there is a husband present or a man acting in the role of husband. This leads to the breakup of the family, pressure on the mother to give up male friends, midnight searches to see if she is harbor-

ing one, and so on. However, in New York City and elsewhere where there is no such requirement, we do not find the critics of welfare satisfied, and proclaiming that all other cities and states need do now is follow the New York model.

3. Welfare leads to further dependency. The children may consider it normal that they grow up to become welfare cases, in particular the girls, and especially where early pregnancy is common. If this is the chief problem, it is extremely difficult to see what any change in the welfare system might do to deal with it.

4. Even if mothers are not required to work and are not required to force out their husbands, qualifying for and remaining on welfare involves many acts that are degrading: attesting to the fact that one has no resources, disposing of certain resources, perhaps giving up the phone and the piano, cooperating with the welfare department in tracking down the absent spouses, and agreeing to support actions against them in court to get funds to support children. Even when support is adequate, it may be argued, these requirements are degrading.

Social Work to Overcome Dependence

In recent years we have seen two major reform movements in welfare, supplementing the earlier emphasis on the need for adequate support, which have addressed themselves to these rather vaguely felt problems of welfare. The first has been the movement to provide counseling, rehabilitation, and work training to welfare clients, as exemplified in the welfare amendments of 1962. The social welfare amendments of 1962 were hailed as the most important revision of welfare since the Social Security Act. They were adopted during the earlier, optimistic years of the Kennedy administration. Kennedy presumably asked the welfare experts, who had lived through a dry decade, what could be done? They wrote revisions of the law, which were adopted—then what happened?

The chief point of the revisions was that the states should be encouraged to do more social work and direct rehabilitation. These amendments have now been in force for several years, and we hear very little about them these days. It would be interesting to know just what the effects of this widely hailed program were. Undoubtedly it gave more work to social workers, but did it get anyone off the rolls? Have the rolls themselves lengthened less rapidly than they might have because of it? Have we learned something about the welfare case families as a result of these experiences? Some experience and knowledge has been accumulated, and it would be valuable to explore it. Public and academic attention, however, have been addressed to the more interesting and exciting domestic programs that have succeeded the welfare amendments: the poverty program, work training programs, Model Cities programs, and so on. At any rate, we can assume, even though I have had no opportunity to examine the experience with the welfare amendments of 1962, that their effects have not been striking.

Welfare Rights

The most recent approach to welfare is that of welfare rights and rights of the poor. This development has certainly been the liveliest one in the welfare field in the last few years. Our evaluation of it depends on what we consider to be the chief problem in welfare. If we consider the chief problem, or a major problem, to be the degradation of the poor, then we will consider this a most important development. Jacobus Ten Broek of the University of California, Berkeley, an expert on constitutional law and a former member of the California State Welfare Board, has argued in an impressive series of articles in the *Stanford Law Review* that there are two systems of law in California, one for those who are well off, and one for those who are poor. The principles of law that hold for the ordinary citizen who is not on welfare oddly enough do not hold if he is on welfare. Thus, there are legal decisions as to the right of one member of the family to support by another, or to have his debts paid by another. The rights of welfare patients in this respect are very different. There are also differences in rules regarding inheritances, rules regarding rights over children, and the like. The argument is interesting but to me unconvincing because all the special rules for the family on welfare derive from a single source: the right of the state to dispense funds for support only on certain conditions, which it sets.

Charles Reich has argued for rights to certain kinds of property, the property of the poor, which means welfare, public housing, and the like; and he has asserted that one should not be deprived of these without the same protection that applies to other property. Various programs granting legal services to the poor have provided lawyers to test rules of administration. They have given the welfare client more opportunity for legal redress, and have increased his power and his dignity.

Aside from these legal developments, there have been political developments, efforts to organize welfare clients to put pressure on welfare agencies. This is reminiscent of the efforts to organize the unemployed in the depression. One such organization, Mothers Against Welfare (MAW), provided the igniting spark for the Roxbury riots in the spring of 1967, when it engaged in a sit-in in the local welfare office.

If one considers one serious problem in welfare to be the deprivation of rights and income by arbitrary officials, then these are valuable and important developments. If one believes too that the increase in the level and expression of discontent by people on welfare is necessary—either that this pressure is required for more generous allotments, for striking fear into the hearts of the administrative officials, or for producing a healthy ferment in the society, or for helping along the revolution—then again, one will consider these legal and political developments valuable. If one considers that the main problem is the size and the growth of the welfare load (namely, the burden of dependency) and how to reduce it, then these new developments simply help to increase the size of welfare rolls and the sums required for the support of the welfare population. On the other hand, they force us to pay closer attention to the reasons for the increase in the welfare rolls.

The increase in AFDC is *the* welfare problem. There has been a striking increase in the numbers of AFDC in New York during the last two years—something like a 40 percent increase—even without an increase in the population, and even though economic conditions have, in general, improved and the level of unemployment has dropped. This is a development that has still not been clarified, and its causes are obscure. I can think of three possibilities; there may be more:

1. The population at risk, in regard to welfare, has been increasing in New York. That is, those with higher incomes and

jobs have been moving out, and young families with children in the low-income groups, prominent among them Negroes and Puerto Ricans, have been coming in. If this is the explanation, why have the welfare rolls in the suburban counties around New York been increasing as rapidly as, or more rapidly than, those in the city?

2. The legal rights and welfare rights movement has been successful in mobilizing as an addition to the welfare rolls many who were eligible but who were not aware of it or who did not opt to go through the process. Thus, in New York there are many more places where information about rights is available to the poor, as a result of the rise of neighborhood and community action programs. There are many more middle-class individuals who are employed in assisting people to get on the rolls, or in overcoming administrative determinations that they are not eligible, or in assisting them to get more once they are on the rolls. (One organization has been distributing lists of the special allotments welfare recipients may receive, and asks those on welfare to check whether they have the winter coat they are eligible for, or the bassinet for the new baby, and the like.) It seems likely this action has served to increase the welfare rolls.

3. Aside from the size of the population at risk, and the impact of movements to increase the proportion of eligibles on welfare, conditions within the population at risk may be changing and leading to an increase in those on welfare, that is, the number of children being born in families without fathers or with fathers with insufficient income may be rising, the number of broken families may be increasing.

Obviously the most important thing for us to understand is this increase in the proportion going on AFDC. Those on welfare have always been only a small proportion of those eligible so the potentiality for growth always existed, and was great; but why did some of the eligibles go onto welfare, and others stay off? Did the latter have hidden resources? Or expect a lower standard of living? Or have deeper cultural resistances to public assistance? I think questions such as these could and should be examined. I suspect ethnic and racial variables are very important here. I would not expect the poor of different racial and ethnic groups to act the same way.

We must do something also to clarify the effects of welfare, if any, and what aspects of welfare have what effects. In

England it was considered very important to eliminate the unpleasant aspects of the means test for social services. This test was felt to involve a stigma. In addition to making people feel bad, it might also single them out, both before the larger public and in their own minds, as members of a special group, and might thus encourage special form of behavior. England and other advanced northwestern countries have done much to eliminate various stigmatizing aspects of social services. How have they done this? With what effects? How does the Englishman who has to resort to National Assistance, because the regular social services are insufficient for his needs, feel about doing so? What kind of problem is National Assistance felt to be?

If we cannot get very far in reducing AFDC by getting mothers to work, how effective would we be in reducing our problem by making it easier for men to work, for presumably it is the man who cannot make a living who abandons his wife and children.

Prospects for the Metropolis

Edward Logue

New York State Urban Development Corporation

Most of us have a personal and somewhat informed judgment of the prospects for the metropolis in which we live and work. Our evaluation of the prospects has guided our decisions about where to live, to work, and to send our children to school. Obviously relatively affluent whites are able to make the most goal-achieving choices, but even relatively low income blacks make choices based on the knowledge of which parts of the metropolitan system are available to them considering their limited resources and the additional limitations that discrimination puts on their freedom of choice. Individually we come to know enough to make choices. We also tend to respond collectively, particularly the white affluents, if the system we have chosen is threatened.

Yet what we know individually, and occasionally respond to in herd fashion, society refuses to acknowledge as the situation.

Example: Suburban schools are better than ghetto schools although state law prescribes uniform standards for public education.

Example: Routine public services within the affluent precincts of the city are performed at a higher level than they are in the ghetto although both statute and political rhetoric demand they be equal.

The list of examples of qualitatively different levels of services within a given metropolitan area can be made as long as the reader will tolerate. Yet the extent of systematic analysis of such differences is limited indeed.

Despite the individual's awareness that these differences exist and guide his personal decisions, society acts out the notion that equality in services is characteristic of the metropolis. All public responsibles defend their services as the equal of any other. Identification with a particular part of the system tends to require a defensive response whatever the facts may be.

Efforts at reform or redressing imbalance are regarded as personal attacks and tend to generate a personal response. (And, in truth, there is some justification for this. When an inner city superintendent of schools is berated for having segregated schools by academics whose children attend suburban or private schools which are predominantly white, one can understand a somewhat sputtering reaction.) Does this perhaps suggest that it would be useful to develop an objective measure of the quality of various public services in various parts of the metropolitan area so that public attention might focus on remedies rather than villains?

Aware individually as we are of what the real situation is, though it be publicly unacknowledged, we are also individually aware that quality of public services is not a constant within the various parts of the metropolis but rather is continually changing and in different ways and at different rates. In fact, perception of the process of change leads to a quantitatively quite significant series of individual (or family) decisions about the best place to live, which has a major impact, in turn, on the prospects for the metropolis.

Yet here again it is almost impossible to get public acknowledgment of varying rates of deterioration or improvement. It is possible to suggest that rates of change in quality of public services and in the characteristics of various parts of the metropolitan area are quantitatively significant enough so that if they represent changes in the cost of living index, national and local attention would inevitably be focused on them.

The absence of any objective measure of conditions in the ghetto relative to the rest of the metropolis denies the society not only a useful analytical tool for developing programs but a warning mechanism that might also be useful. A Metropolitan

Services Index (MSI) could be developed through the PPBS approach for a given metropolis within a reasonably short period of time. Its extension to other metropolitan areas would provide interesting opportunities to observe significant variations across the country. (For example, most urban observers primarily familiar with eastern ghettos are startled to find that the Watts area has a relatively benign appearance compared with Harlem.)

The quality of public service is improving in affluent areas and declining in ghetto areas, and this trend is no secret, though not publicly acknowledged. How much does this spreading gap contribute to increased militancy and/or alienation in the ghetto and to increasing pessimism or hostility in affluent areas to efforts aimed at redressing the balance? Many other questions arise. If the trends are identifiable for each significant metropolitan area, what can we learn about such things as the dates when center city school systems will have an irreversible imbalance of Negro children in the public schools, or of Negro voters on the voting lists?

The availability of an accepted MSI for a series of metropolitan areas should inform the coming debate on metropolitan government. It might retard or accelerate the trend toward proliferation of federal categorical grant programs. It might encourage the state level of government to decide that there was (or was not) a politically viable way of dealing with inequalities in areas that have long been regarded as the province of state and local government rather than the federal government. It might help the private sector to understand its perhaps unwitting role in increasing rather than eliminating the gap. It might help the ghetto community to focus more precisely on program goals. It might discourage the use of rhetoric without resources, exhortation without incentive, and so on.

The MSI area should be identical with the SMSA. Using census data it should establish various categories to denote recognizably different parts of the standard metropolitan statistical area (SMSA). One possible set of MSI area categories is the following:

Affluent suburb
Average suburb
Affluent neighborhood
Average city neighborhood

Transition city neighborhood

Ghetto

Many different sets of public services are possible candidates for measurement:

Housing—Is the housing in generally good, bad, improving, or deteriorating condition? What is the public service response?

Education—Is the school system esteemed or isn't it?

Personal safety—Are there commonly used parts of the environment not regarded as safe? To whom? When?

Routine public services—Is the public environment kempt?

Recreation—Are recreation facilities available in quantity and variety and with what level of maintenance?

Transportation—Does the transportation system facilitate journeys to work?

Revenue—Is the revenue base being improved or eroded?

Rapport—Is there reasonable rapport or hostility (covert or otherwise) between citizen and public employee?

Racial balance[1]—Is the trend toward a majority of nonwhite residents in the area?

The rating system can be numerical, alphabetical, or what have you. Since our system is still in a primitive state, we will use a simple Pass/Fail rating system. This sample MSI trend index for one hypothetical SMSA may encourage the reader to rate his own.

	Affluent suburb	Average suburb	Affluent neighborhood	Average neighborhood	Changing neighborhood	Ghetto
Housing	P	P	P	F	F	F
Education	P	P	P	P—	F	F
Personal and public safety	P	P	P	P—	F	F
Routine public services	P	P—	P—	P—	F	F
Recreation	P	P	F	P	F	F
Transportation	P	P—	P	P—	F	F
Revenue	P	F	P	F	F	F
Rapport	P	P	P	?	F	F
Racial balance	F	F	F	P	F	F

[1] Not perhaps a public service category, but it seems to belong.

The MSI is not pejorative. It does not single out villains. It may objectively show patterns and thus perhaps point the way to priorities. It may also raise questions about the value of over-categorized approaches and of demonstration projects. It may even manage to raise the question of scale. It can be useful in evaluating alternative approaches to improving the quality of particular public services while reminding us that attention to one function without attention to others may limit achievement.

With the MSI we may now have established in an objective way, simplistic perhaps but striking, the marked inequality of education and other services within our SMSA. It might be interesting to proceed now to a simplistic effort to design systems that will eliminate these inequalities.

Human Resource Expenditures: Investment or Redistribution?

Burton A. Weisbrod

University of Wisconsin

If public programs are to come to grips with the problems of cities, we must first clarify fundamental issues and concepts with regard to defining and evaluating the role of the federal government in the human resource field. This paper[1] considers one such issue, the relevance of economic efficiency as compared with other considerations in the evaluation of human resource programs. The paper is addressed primarily to persons other than professional economists; to the latter group, much of the argument is familiar, while part will be found to be incompletely developed in this brief presentation.

The term *human resources* carries the connotation that people may be viewed as productive assets, assets in which investments may be made and from which tangible, salable returns may be expected. This analogy of government investments, whether directly in people or in nonhuman forms, with ordinary business investment has much to commend it, since resource scarcity compels us to make choices with regard to public as well as private expenditures; but—and here is the simple theme of this paper—the analogy would be carried too far if one were to conclude that income-distributional consider-

[1] The author would like to thank Glen Cain, W. Lee Hansen, and Robert J. Lampman for their valuable comments on an earlier draft.

ations and other social goals were irrelevant for *government* expenditure policy, simply because they may be disregarded by *private* investors. Such goals are germane to all government expenditures, but they are likely to loom especially large for programs involving human resources.

There is some empirical evidence that expenditures on human resources, particularly through education, are profitable investments. Formal schooling, for example, appears to be profitable in the sense that, on average, the increase in productivity (earnings) apparently attributable to schooling exceeds the estimated costs of that schooling. Within very recent years, however, evidence has been growing that although education may be a socially and privately profitable investment in general, it may not be profitable, at least in the business-investment sense, for groups such as those high school students who are seriously contemplating dropping out of school, children from seriously underprivileged backgrounds, and people of low ability.[2] That is, the social costs of educational programs for these groups frequently appear to exceed the benefits in the form of increased earnings. To be sure, there may be benefits, to students and to others ("external" benefits), in addition to increased productivity; yet at present we can do little more than speculate about their importance.

Thus we confront an important issue: *if* certain public expenditures are to be justified on the grounds that they represent profitable investments, should such expenditures be made when they are *not* "profitable"? To illustrate, assume that government preventive health expenditures are profitable investments, in general. Would they also be profitable if made on behalf of the health of aged people? Because the aged are normally retired, hence contribute little to output of the economy (at least as measured), it is apparent that expenditures on their behalf would not be shown to be profitable investments in the usual sense. Does it follow that there should be no public expenditures devoted to the health of retired people?

Another example: In general, a high school education ap-

[2] See, for examples, Thomas Ribich, "Education and Poverty," unpublished manuscript submitted to The Brookings Institution, Washington, D.C., 1968; Burton A. Weisbrod, "Preventing High School Dropouts," in Robert Dorfman, ed., *Measuring Benefits of Government Investments* (Washington, D.C.: The Brookings Institution, 1965); and W. Lee Hansen, Burton A. Weisbrod, and William Scanlon, "Determinants of Earnings: Does Schooling Really Count?" University of Wisconsin, Economics of Human Resources Working Paper 5, December, 1967.

pears to be a profitable public investment. It could be true, however, that for persons such as Negroes, who are victimized by discrimination, expenditures on high school education are not profitable because the Negro graduates would be unable to obtain jobs normally obtainable by white graduates. Consequently, high school education might actually return little, either in increased productivity for the economy or in increased earnings for the individual. If this were true, should we devote public resources to high school education for Negroes? Illustrations of this sort could be multiplied many times.

Or, to turn the example around, what if it were determined that public expenditures on undergraduate education at some Ivy League college would be efficient (that is, profitable) investments in the sense that students' future productivity (as measured by earnings) would be increased by considerably more than the added cost; ought we to favor public subsidy for these students—students who tend to have above-average ability, come from families with above-average affluence, and who are already receiving college education of above-average quality?

The point is that government expenditures, and especially human resource expenditures, may be made because they are expected to increase productivity, or they may be made for quite different reasons. We might spend on health for the aged simply because we regard this as desirable, notwithstanding the lack of effect on measured output. We might devote resources to education even though there were no demonstrable effect on the output or earning capacity of the individuals involved. We might refrain from making an "efficient" investment if the beneficiaries were an already privileged group. In short, there are many social goals for which we strive other than that of increasing economic output. We must face up to the possibility that investments in human resources may not always be as efficient in raising measured output as are alternative investments. We may make the investments in people anyway.

Economists have had little to say about the desirability of expenditures when considerations other than economic efficiency are involved. Thus, the empirical work on benefit-cost analysis in the human resources area has largely emphasized the effects of such programs on national product, that is, it has emphasized the investment-efficiency character of expenditures. It has paid virtually no attention to the income-distributional effects of those expenditures, or to their contribution to other social goals. The federal government, in particular, however, should consider the effects of its actions not only on the size of economic output, but also on the distribution—and on the manner in which the distribution (or redistribution) is brought about. Moreover, the federal government must consider the effects of its programs on other goals, such as "equality of opportunity," which may have only an indirect or remote connection with measured aggregate economic output.

This state of events provides a basis for concern. The "human resources" approach involves looking at people as productive assets. It follows from this point of view that certain activities should be undertaken insofar as they will contribute to the productivity of resources; at the same time, this point of view seems to suggest, although not to imply logically, that certain activities should be forgone unless they will contribute to productivity by more than the cost of the resources used.

But economic efficiency (as customarily measured) is only one of the goals government decision-makers should seek, and it is very important that attention be given to the tradeoffs among goals, to the tradeoffs that society is *willing* to make and to those that it is *able* to make. Only when this is done will we be able to decide intelligently how many resources ought to go into expanding output as compared with redistributing that output or contributing to other social objectives. In any event, we do need to face up to the easy error that accompanies an oversimplified application of the human resources approach, the error of deciding that resources should be devoted *only* to those programs for which productivity benefits exceed cost.

At the same time, we must not disregard economic efficiency. Our judgment about the wisdom of, for example, a manpower retraining program versus a pure transfer payment program to aid the long-term unemployed might well be very different depending on whether it were estimated that the (present value of) increased earnings resulting from the retraining amounted to, say, 90 percent, or only 20 percent of the resource costs. Society might feel that the advantages of enabling people to earn a living—this might be one social goal—were such that the training program should be supported if there is a social return of even 90 percent of costs. But if the return were only 20 percent, then it might be felt that a simple cash transfer would be preferable.

The danger in an uncritical application of business-investment criteria to government expenditures in general, and to human resource expenditures in particular—that is, the danger of emphasizing economic efficiency and essentially disregarding income-distributional and other effects—comes into sharp focus when one is considering programs to raise productivity and earning capacity for the disadvantaged, including the poor, the long-term unemployed, the uneducated, and so on. Viewing these programs as investments in human resources, government agencies have increasingly labored to estimate benefit-cost ratios or similar measures of economic efficiency. When benefits, at least in the form of increased expected earnings, have appeared to be less than costs, disappointment has followed.

Should one have seriously expected another outcome? Probably not. The fact that the group was "disadvantaged" suggests that raising its earnings would not be easy or cheap; and the fact that the private market had not operated to provide training programs, special trade schools, placement services and the like is further evidence, though only of a presumptive sort, that raising earnings will be costly. It is true, of course, that lack of information and other sources of market imperfection could be at fault, or there might be important benefits from such programs to persons other than the direct beneficiaries. Yet what needs to be known is whether such imperfections or external benefits are more significiant in the markets for the disadvantaged than they are in other sectors. They may be, but the question needs to be explored further. As a first approximation we should not expect that investments will be "efficient," in the business-investment sense, when aimed at people with whom the private market has chosen not to act, whether those people are disadvantaged or not. (To be sure, as with all presumptions, this one is also subject to refutation.)

I do not conclude that government investments for the disadvantaged are undesirable, only that they are quite likely to be economically inefficient, in some degree; that is, productivity benefits are likely to fall short of costs. Justification for such programs will depend, therefore, on evidence of unusually great market imperfections or external social benefits, or, very often, on concerns about income-distributional or other social welfare objectives.

In the development of public policy in the human resources area, there are two dangers to be avoided: (1) we should not apply straightforward business-investment (economic efficiency) criteria for assessing program desirability—in particular, we should not disregard income-distributional effects; but (2) neither should we allow our concern about income distribution and other social goals to soften our resolve to improve the quality of benefit-cost analyses.

Urban Violence and Public Order

The Problems of Urban Ghettos and the Issues of Public Order

Seymour Martin Lipset

Harvard University

The emergence of riots in the urban ghettos is seemingly a new situation as far as the Negroes in the United States are concerned. A detailed survey of the condition of the American Negro, published in 1964, discusses various possibilities, but does not even mention the possibilities of Negro riots. The literature bearing on the problems of interracial violence, other than crime, dealt with white violence against Negroes in the form of lynchings or race riots. Whites had attacked Negro areas during and after World War I. The Detroit race riot of 1943 was a white riot. Whites engaged in violence to keep Negroes out of previously all-white neighborhoods or schools during the 1950s and 1960s.

The change in the situation in 1965 was occasioned by a number of factors. Perhaps the two most relevant events were the reemergence of a white-based student radical movement, which had taken over the tactics of civil disobedience from the southern civil rights movement, and had dramatized in various ways that authority could be intimidated by such tactics, and the growth of black nationalism within the Negro community. The latter, though a minority phenomenon, attested to the fact that the promise of equality was beginning to appear hollow to many Negro activists and intellectuals. It also constituted a reaction to the fact that much of the ideological justification for integration was premised on the proposition that white culture is good, black is bad, and the only way that blacks can improve their situation is to lose themselves in a crowd of whites, particularly in the schools.

From a long-term point of view, however, the growth in alienated behavior on the part of the Negroes is a function of the fact that various political events had committed the society to the promise of equality more strongly than ever before. The 1948 civil rights platform of the Democratic party, which resulted in a Dixiecrat walkout, and which, in any event, was not enacted by Congress, promised much less in the way of civil rights than was obtained in the decade from 1954 to 1964. But in spite of the various judicial decisions and the passage of strong civil rights legislation on the national level, and of even broader laws in many northern states, the social and economic reality of the American Negro remains brutal. As he finally seeks to enter American society with the government and various other powerful institutions seemingly strongly behind him, he finds the doors closed because of an ironic twist of fate. The present economy is one that is increasingly characterized as having *plenty of room at the top but no room at the bottom.* There is a growing need for educated, trained people, but little need for muscle power and unskilled work. This is the exact opposite of the situation in the nineteenth and early twentieth centuries, when European immigrants were entering the occupational structure. Then millions of Europeans and others came into the United States seeking employment; and, though many faced discrimination, there were many job vacancies for the unskilled. The most rapidly growing part of the occupational structure involved unskilled and semiskilled jobs, positions anyone with any degree of motivation to work could secure.

Today, in order to enter the expanding parts of the social and economic structure, the majority of Negroes must jump from a low level of education and skill, and a low achievement motivation, to a high level. The cultural residues of slavery and caste inferiority, which have been abundantly documented in studies of the family and education, prevent many of them from doing so. The result is that the Negro finds that he has been given a phony check or a false promise, that the civil rights legislation does little good in providing decent jobs or housing. Even the accrediting mechanisms of society operate to increase the sense of frustration since Negroes in southern and ghetto schools often are given formal claims to position in the form of high school diplomas and college degrees, which do not mean the same thing as they do for whites. There is still an amazingly high percentage of Negroes with college education who are employed in manual work, not necessarily because of discrimination. Relatively few Negroes are available to take jobs as engineers, as highly skilled technicians, as members of college faculties—the kinds of jobs which are expanding rapidly.

This situation, in which the civil rights movement has won almost all the victories it ever hoped to achieve politically and yet Negro unemployment is as great *relative* to the total economy as it has ever been, clearly makes for great frustration, particularly among unemployed and young Negroes. It is easy to understand why the context of tremendous promise and little positive *real* results produces increasing bitterness, alienation, greater violence, and greater lawlessness. Both Tocqueville and Marx in the nineteenth century pointed out that factors that resulted in heightening what we now call relative deprivation are more important in producing receptivity for revolution than intense, but stable, objective deprivation. Stable poverty, as Durkheim tried to document, is more likely to result in conservatism than protest and radicalism.

There are, of course, other elements that press in the same direction. Studies of protests and riots in the nineteenth and twentieth centuries have noted that dislocations of social positions brought about by industrialization and urbanization heighten the potential for extreme mass behavior. Thus workers and urban dwellers relatively recently recruited from rural populations are more likely to support political extremism than those who are native to an urban industrial culture. Those who have broken their ties to the social structures in which they were reared, who have left friends and kin, are receptive to new ideologies, values, and demagogic appeals. New religions and protest movements arise among those who are uncommitted to institutions because of migration. The Ku Klux Klan and the Black Legion recruited during the 1920s and 1930s from white workers in the cities who had recently migrated from the South. Research which I have done on the Klan in urban areas in the 1920s indicates a correlation between Klan strength and the rate of growth of cities. Similar patterns occur among middle-class extremists. Birch Society support is significantly greater among relatively recent migrants to cities, and in rapidly growing communities.

There is another special aspect of the structure of ghetto and slum areas which affects the number available for "action," and that is the school dropout rate among teen-agers. The various reports on Negro unemployment point out that it is concentrated heavily among teen-agers; the estimates run as high as 25 percent. To a considerable degree, these are youth who have never had a steady position. Youth generally are more "irresponsible" than adults in a noninvidious sense. That is, they are less involved in the responsibilities imposed by career and family. Adolescent subculture also often tends to emphasize the virtues of courage, or risk-taking. Reports on riots and revolts in various parts of the world have pointed to the role of youth in taking daring actions. The situation of untrained lower-class youth today is somewhat different from the past because of the effect of minimum wage legislation. It sometimes does not "pay" employers to hire unskilled youth at the minimum wage. In earlier periods, school leavers were often criticized for taking jobs away from married fathers of families because youth would take jobs at lower wage rates than heads of families could afford. Hence, today, the Negro unemployed consist largely of those who are most prone of all age groups to engage in extreme actions.

A relevant finding of political sociology which seems at first glance to run counter to the discussion of youth is one that reports that the unemployed and the down and out are less likely to support or join radical groups than those who are employed, but were previously unemployed. Thus various studies of the unemployed in different countries during the depression of the 1930s point out that the unemployed showed a decline in levels of reading radical literature, attendance at political meetings, and membership in radical organizations as compared with when they had been employed. The typical behavior pattern of the unemployed workers is to retreat from all forms of social participation, to become passive and apathetic. During upswings in the business cycle, however, those who had been unemployed have shown greater propensities to support extreme radical groups than those who have never been unemployed. As a result of research in the Bedford-Stuyvesant area of Brooklyn, Gerald Schaflander and others report similar patterns among adult Negroes. Those who are most depressed economically are least involved in any form of protest organization, and have little knowledge about what is going on in militant Negro groups. Among adults, therefore, it might be argued that the greatest militancy should be found among employed individuals who once were in a more deprived state. Among youth, however, the same generalization need not apply. Negro teen-agers who were never employed and who do not have family responsibilities presumably should not experience the same kind of individual depression that occurs among people who have lost jobs or who have greater responsibilities. Thus one might expect to find adults with positions taking part in extreme forms of protest together with unemployed youth.

If factors such as those discussed above have affected the propensity of the slum dwelling population to be disposed and available for extreme or violent action, the mass media, particularly through the widespread diffusion of television and radio coverage of events, have contributed to spreading the sparks which initially kindle active unrest. I was in Berlin in June, 1953, during the uprising in East Berlin. This uprising began with a building workers' strike on June 16 which resulted in a number of spontaneous discussion meetings in the streets of the city. RIAS (Radio in the American Sector), which reached out all over East Germany, sent recording trucks into East Berlin, and recorded speeches and interviews with various militants. These speeches and interviews were then rebroadcast repeatedly. On June 17, there were 100,000 people in the downtown areas of East Berlin, and strikes all over the Soviet Zone. The quick buildup of the protest in Berlin and its spread through the Zone was clearly a result of radio. Similarly in Watts in 1965, one television channel was on the air for 24 hours covering the riot by various means including helicopters which descended over the looting and other actions. James Q. Wilson reports in *The Public Interest* having been in a car in the Negro district of Albany as a riot broke out. A reporter for the local Negro music station (there is now one in almost every city) was in a car in front of him, and broadcast a highly dramatic version of what was happening. Wilson notes that as he watched, he could see people pouring out of houses, bars, stores, and so on, clearly in response to the radio reports. To cite an earlier example of the same process, in 1939, the Nazi German-American Bund held a rally in Madison Square Garden. A small Trotskyist group, the Socialist Workers Party, with at most a few hundred members in New York City, called for a protest demonstration outside the Garden. The Trotskyists by themselves could have not reached more than some thousands of people. The *New York Daily News,* with its multimillion circulation, however, reproduced the Trotskyist leaflet calling for the protest on its front page. As a result there were close to 100,000 people outside the Garden that night.

The mass media can affect the likelihood of mass actions through means other than coverage of specific events. Their decision to report on the comments and activities of small groups of extremists or their spokesmen enable these groups to reach out to those in the larger community or the nation who are sympathetic. What is a tiny minority in percentage terms can become an effective mass group in absolute numbers. The problem of such minority groups is to find the others who agree with them. One reason that activist student groups are so effective is that the campus is one of the few communities in which all those with common opinions can be easily reached, often simply by giving out leaflets or putting up posters. The 1 or 2 percent of the 25,000 students who might be sympathetic to a given demonstration are relatively easily mobilized. In the community at large, this cannot be done except with the help of the media. When the media give time or space to a George Wallace or a Rap Brown, they enable them to find their potential supporters. Thus, I am convinced that the rapid growth in the Wallace for President movement reflected the decision of the media, particularly the press, to give him major candidate coverage. How does this process occur? In one weekend, November 12, 1967, four papers I read carried a long story on Wallace: the *New York Times,* the *Washington Post,* the *Christian Science Monitor,* and the (London) *Observer.* These stories were not in response to any given event or speech, but rather were reports on the Wallace campaign and the content of his speeches. I cannot believe that coverage of this sort is purely spontaneous, the result of four independent decisions. I have been told by journalists that when one important outlet decides to cover a given event or report, the others feel pressed to do the same. Former Governor Edmund S. Brown and others in California have suggested that the widespread coverage on TV and in the press of the most dramatic events on the Berkeley campus during the 1964–65 "Student Revolt" contributed to making the Watts riots possible. There is no way of knowing whether this is so or not, but I would guess that the general assumptions concerning the diffusion of tactics, attitudes toward law and order, ideas, and the like through the mass media are valid.

To turn to another topic, I think it is important to recognize, in reacting to recent forms of mass violence in America, that the patterns involved are not unique to situations of racial tension, or to the contemporary world. Mass riots originating in depressed areas in large cities have occurred elsewhere. In the summer of 1967 there was a major riot in the slums of Tokyo. The police station in the center of the slums of Osaka is built like a fortress, to withstand riots, of which there have been a number in recent years. Slum riots have occurred frequently in Calcutta and other Indian cities. Going back in European history, one may find evidence of many urban riots. London was swept by the Gordon riots in the late eighteenth century. There were riots during the next 50 years in various parts of the country. The poor of Paris took part in a number of riots during the revolutionary years. Riots occurred frequently in American cities during the nineteenth century. Protestant mobs roamed a number of cities in various periods before the Civil War destroying Catholic institutions and districts. The Irish, in turn, engaged in riots, of which the most noteworthy were the antidraft riots during the Civil War. As I noted earlier, anti-Negro riots occurred in many places between World Wars I and II. Few of these riots were a product of, or resulted in, continuing protest movements. It is important, therefore, both to look at the sources and pattern of events which occurred in these riot situations, and to evaluate the implications of the present ones without exaggeration. They may or may not be portents of a continuing tendency to rely on violence to attain the ends of the Negro community. It is important, for example, to note in this regard that all the studies of Negro ghetto opinion indicate that the vast majority are much more concerned with inadequate policing in the ghetto than with anti-Negro actions by the police.

The violent tactics of many Negroes today must be placed in the context, which many have been doing, of the American propensity to seek to attain ends regardless of the means employed. The United States has by far the highest rate of law violation, and particularly of homicide, of any developed Protestant nation. Various American social movements, including the labor movement, have shown considerable propensity in the past to rely on violence to attain their ends. It has been pointed out that American unions, though relatively conservative in their ideology as compared with European unions, have been among the most militant of unions around the world in terms of tactics. They have used dynamite, arson, and sit-ins as weapons against employers. They have made alliances with the underworld to attain their ends. The "conservative" white South has relied on civil and uncivil disobedience to hold down the Negro for more than a century. I have discussed some of the sources of the propensity to violence in my book, *The First New Nation,* and I will not repeat them here. I would simply note in this regard that reliance on violence and political radicalism are not coterminous in America, that elements in our value system and social structure seem to encourage a variety of groups to use illegitimate means to attain their objectives.

As a final relevant comment, I would note that American history reveals a propensity for the rise of short-lived social movements, which often have involved millions of persons in their actitiies. While such movements existed, various analysts explained their rise as a result of basic endemic tension-creating social processes, explanations which implied that the movements should continue to exist and even grow. Yet almost all of them declined rapidly within a few years after arising. To list some of these will indicate what I have in mind.

The Anti-Masons arose in 1826 following the murder of a former Mason who was about to publish a book exposing supposed Masonic plots. The movement charged that the country faced a vast danger, and engaged in lawlessness, elected governors in Pennsylvania and Vermont, came close to electing one in New York, had over 150 members of the Massachusetts House, and published over 150 newspapers. Its heyday in terms of strength was from 1828 to 1832. Various efforts to revive anti-Masonry have been attempted from then on down to the present with little success.

A variety of anti-Catholic and nativist riots and movements occurred from the 1840s to the 1920s. The largest pre-Civil War movement, the Know-Nothings or American party, had a period of considerable strength and won elections in many states from 1854 to 1857, then quickly dwindled away. The American Protective Association of the 1890s is reported to have had millions of members. It began in 1886, but basically had its greatest strength between 1893 and 1896, and almost totally disappeared thereafter. The Ku Klux Klan is reputed to have had from three to six million members in the 1920s. It also elected many governors and other officials. Its period of greatest support was between 1921 and 1925. By the late twenties, it was a small group. On the left, one may point to the Populists (1890–1896) and the Socialist party, which secured 6 percent of the national vote in 1912, and had well over 100,000 members at the time. Both declined quickly. The 1930s witnessed the growth of a variety of movements, of which the two largest were Huey Long's Share-Our-Wealth Movement, and the Coughlinite National Union for Social Justice. Opinion surveys gave Long and Coughlin a considerable following. Long's totally vanished with his assassination in 1935; his second-in-command, Gerald L. K. Smith, could not find a handful to follow him. A Coughlinite movement remained until World War II, but then also vanished into limbo. Opinion survey data from 1935 through the end of World War II indicate that a considerable amount of fairly virulent anti-Semitism existed among American Christians. Yet all the postwar studies suggest that such sentiments declined rapidly after the war, and have remained at a low ebb. The same is true for the anti-Japanese feeling on the West Coast. McCarthyism lasted four years, from 1950–1954. The White Citizen's Councils have been declining since they reached their high point in 1964. The Birch Society, a much smaller group, apparently had its zenith in terms of membership and support about 1965, and has been losing members and splintering since. On the left the LaFollette Progressive party secured 17 percent of the vote in 1924, the largest ever secured by a group to the left of the Democrats, and disappeared as an effort soon thereafter. The Garveyite Negro nationalist movement was very strong during the 1920s but also dwindled quickly.

Looking over this record suggests the need to locate not only why and when different groups of Americans become disposed to form and join movements far outside the American "consensus," but why they decline so quickly. Some of them, for example, the Anti-Masons, lose out after seemingly achieving their most prominent objective. Many others splinter because they include many who differ widely on issues other than the main one that brought them into existence. Others have lost out after revelations that their leaders were involved in fradulent activities, or after they began to fight among themselves, or died. But whatever the proximate cause of decline, what is most interesting is that the strains that seemingly had led millions to join or follow these movements did not lead them to back others subsequently. There is no secular tendency connected with any of them.

I do not want to suggest that any necessary conclusions about the duration of any of the current patterns of protest on either the right or the left can be deduced from the fact that their predecessors have been so short-lived. Clearly, no one has presented an adequate causal explanation that can be applied to the contemporary scene. But on the other hand, it is important to be aware of this history before concluding that things will be different this time. There are, of course, a few general statements that can be made about the sources of failure of many, though not all, of these past movements. First, those that have tried the "third party" route have invariably faced the constraints placed on such efforts by the American constitutional structure, which makes of the entire country one constituency for the one important election, that of the presidency. Reasonably successful third parties are usually pressed to give up because one of the major parties offers them a coalition in the form of candidates or ideology, which party leaders or their followers find difficult to resist. The movements, as distinct from the parties, often attract leaders and activists whose values and personalities make it difficult for them to compromise on new issues facing the movement. The intense factional struggles that quickly arise result in such acrimonious backbiting as to discourage the bulk of the membership. Those movements that have engaged in violence and are taken over by the more extreme elements within them often find the more moderate groups withdrawing. The "Establishment" often turns against large extreme movements in ways that also discourage the more moderate supporters from remaining with them. Many of these movements have attracted conscious charlatans, who seek to use the movement for very narrow personal purposes (money and sex have been the most notable), and are thus made vulnerable to exposure, which discourages their idealistic followers. But whatever the cause of decline, the fact remains that all such efforts have quickly subsided. They often have been responsible for a great deal of good and evil in the form of legislation or new institutions, but the one thing they have never been able to do is to institutionalize their alienated patterns of response to the body politic. And their use of violence has never led to the continuation of such tactics as a normal method of politics.

Recommendations for Analysis and Action

On the broadest level, there are two major recommendations: the first is to do all that is possible to integrate the Negro community into the economy, society, and polity. The second is to have patience and fortitude, and not get excited over the problems of riots and the seeming growth of political extremism.

Integration clearly involves a considerable degree of planning and a high level of public expenditures to eliminate unemployment and slum housing conditions. To raise a few specifics, there is a clear need to subsidize the employment of young and unskilled people, through paying employers part of their wages for some initial training period. Subsidization is the only politic and morale sustaining way of pressing private employers to hire many Negroes. Any massive effort to tackle the problem of slum housing and facilities should also include provisions for hiring workers from the areas in which new housing and facilities are being built.

On the research side, someone should make an intensive study of wartime hiring experiences. During World War II, various defense industries hired hundreds of thousands of untrained people on cost-plus contracts. How successful were they in really training them and incorporating them into the industrial work milieu? To point to an interesting concrete case, the Kaiser shipyards in Richmond, California, hired close to 100,000 new workers, mainly Negroes and whites from the South, in one year, 1942–43. These people were housed in new defense housing in the city. At the time, the various government agencies involved assumed that these workers would lose their jobs and leave the area after the war ended. In fact, labor market studies for 1948 through 1950 revealed that very few left, that almost all of them had found new positions in the Bay Area.

To incorporate the slums into the polity also requires some conscious action. Basically what is needed is to involve them in real political structures. The notion of local "city halls" is a step in this direction. The Alinsky efforts at creating movements are another way to deal with the problem. How successful are the latter? What is called for to answer this question is some systematic research on the structure of participation, representation, knowledge, and awareness in the slum communities. Nothing really good has been done on this subject.

Other measures have been suggested bearing on the problem of the potential for riots. One of the reasons the summer is the season of riots is that school is out, that many youth, who are basically not in the labor market, are free and have little to do. The suggestion that schools stay open 12 months a year is directed to this problem. Conceivably, schools could stay open as centers of special training, in which participants would be paid to attend. They also could be used as community centers. Older youth could be hired for the summer to run athletic and other programs for younger ones. Such programs should be started on an experimental basis right away.

The patience and fortitude suggestion is premised on the assumption that the emergence of riots and extremism at any point in time does not necessarily imply a secular or continuing pattern. A more detailed knowledge of the phenomenon of riots in a comparative and historical context would be most helpful in planning how to react to them.

Bibliography

I have touched on a number of these topics in various of my writings, especially *Political Man* (Garden City: Doubleday-Anchor, 1960); *The First New Nation* (New York: Basic Books, 1963, and Doubleday-Anchor, 1967); *Society and Politics* (New York: Basic Books, 1968) and in a book which Earl Raab and I are now writing on "right-wing extremism in historical perspective." A number of books have been written on specific anti-Negro riots from the St. Louis and Chicago riots around World War I to the Detroit riots of

1943. On American values and their propensity to press men to violate the rules of the game, see Robert K. Merton, *Social Theory and Social Structure* (New York: The Free Press, 1957), especially Chapters IV and V, pp. 121–194; Daniel Bell, *The End of Ideology* (New York: The Free Press, 1960), especially the chapters on "Crime," pp. 115–158; and some chapters in *The First New Nation,* 5, "Trade Unions and the American Value System," and 7, "Value Differences . . . ," especially pp. 262–270; and in *Society and Politics,* especially chapter 3, "Revolution and Counter-Revolution, The United States and Canada." On the strains contributing to the rise of social movements and group violence, see Neil Smelser, *A Theory of Collective Behavior* (Chicago: University of Chicago Press, 1963). On the pre-riots situation, politics, and attitudes of Negroes, see Thomas Pettigrew, *A Profile of the Negro American* (Princeton: D. Van Nostrand Co., 1964); James Q. Wilson, *Negro Politics* (New York: The Free Press, 1960); Harry A. Bailey, Jr., ed., *Negro Politics in America* (Columbus: Charles E. Merrill, 1967); Gary Marx, *Protest and Prejudice: A Study of Belief in the Black Community* (New York: Harper and Row, 1967); William Brink and Louis Harris, *The Negro Revolution in America* (New York: Simon and Shuster, 1964). A recent compendium containing reports on a number of these topics is Kenneth Clark and Talcott Parsons eds., *The Negro American* (Boston: Houghton Mifflin, 1967). On the role of the very deprived, see James Davies, "Towards a Theory of Revolution," *American Sociological Review* (February, 1962); B. Zawadski and P. F. Lazarsfeld, "The Psychological Consequences of Unemployment," *Journal of Social Psychology* (May, 1935); and S. M. Lipset, *Political Man, The Social Basis of Politics* (Garden City: Doubleday-Anchor, 1959), pp. 232–236.

On the effect of economic growth, urbanization, and geographic mobility on propensity for extremism, see William Kornhauser, *The Politics of Mass Society* (Glencoe: The Free Press, 1959), pp. 145 and passim; S. M. Lipset, *Political Man,* pp. 68–71; S. M. Lipset, "The Changing Class Structure and Contemporary European Politics," in S. Graubard, ed., *A New Europe?* (Boston: Houghton Mifflin, 1964), pp. 355–356; John C. Leggett, "Uprootedness and Working-Class Consciousness," *American Journal of Sociology,* 68 (1963), pp. 683–692; Mancur Olson, Jr., "Rapid Growth as a Destabilizing Force," *Journal of Economic History,* 27 (1963), pp. 529–552; Bert Hoselitz and Myron Weiner, "Economic Development and Political Stability in India," *Dissent,* 8 (spring, 1961), pp. 172–179. On the political propensities of students and young people, see the various articles collected in S. M. Lipset, ed., *Student Politics* (New York: Basic Books, 1967), and in the issue of *Daedalus* dealing with "Students and Politics," 97 (winter, 1968).

Black Nationalism and Prospects for Violence in the Ghetto

Guy J. Pauker

The Rand Corporation

We have witnessed an acceleration of the revolutionary process in the black community in the last two or three years. Of course there is a time lag between the state of mind of the most militant leaders and that of the masses whom they are trying to draw along with them. In discussing prospects for violence in the ghetto, the most important question to be asked is whether the rate of radicalization of the black masses is still slow enough to allow time for the implementation of measures that would arrest the trend toward making the militant leadership the controlling, dominant political force of the black movement. It has been argued that the payoffs expected by the black population are monetary, not ideological. Would material payoffs really prompt the masses to ignore the militant leaders?

I have no reliable answers to these crucial questions, but I would like to present a point of view which might broaden the frame within which the problem of black unrest is being considered. There is no question that black-initiated riots have increased in numbers in the last few years. A Legislative Reference Service report on civil disorder shows that before November, 1962, riots involving race clashes were initiated by whites who beat up blacks or civil rights workers. The first black-initiated riot took place in November, 1962, after a football game in Washington, D.C., where black students beat up white spectators and policemen.[1] After that date riots are dominantly black-initiated, and their number increases every year.

It is interesting, or perhaps sobering, to note how incapable social scientists are of anticipating events. In *The Negro American,* which Kenneth Clark edited with Talcott Parsons in 1965 when the militant black movement was already a reality, he wrote in the introduction:

> . . . the use of force for the maintenance of class, racial, economic, or national distinctions is no longer tolerable or possible. The revulsion against international war has infected the domestic society, as well, and we are no longer willing to allow violence to be the determinant of status in American society. . . . The strategy of nonviolence reflects most obviously the fact that Negroes, in the minority, could not afford to be violent—except for the unplanned Watts type of violence, itself suicidal or a reflection of racial desperation.[2]

Talcott Parsons, in his introduction to the same volume, wrote:

> The principal counter to pessimism . . . lies in the strength of a *combination* of factors which have already begun to promote inclusion, and which almost certainly will be greatly strengthened in the coming years, unless the main developmental trend of the society is unexpectedly interrupted.
>
> Not the least of these factors [which militate against the use of violence in American society] is the civil rights movement itself . . . [which is of a] legally acceptable type of civil disobedience . . . "non-violent," "symbolic," "aimed at the conscience." This formula can perhaps be generalized to characterize the role of the movement as a whole. Particularly in the accelerating phase of the last five years, it has provided, along with the Supreme Court, the most important link between the moral values which Myrdal emphasized and the present processes of implementation of those values.[3]

[1] *Special Report: Urban Problems and Civil Disorder, Congressional Quarterly Weekly,* no. 36 (September 8, 1967), p. 1709.

[2] Talcott Parsons, and Kenneth B. Clark, *The Negro American* (Boston: Beacon Press, 1967), p. xvi.

[3] *Ibid.,* p. xxv.

Parsons was, of course, referring to Gunnar Myrdal's *American Dilemma.* Let me move to the other side of the track and quote. Stokely Carmichael from a book he and Charles V. Hamilton, a black political scientist, published in August, 1967:

> . . . in a profit-oriented, materialistic society, there is little time to reflect on creeds, especially if it could mean more job competition, "lower property values," and "the daughter marrying a Negro." There is no "American dilemma," no moral hang-up, and black people should not base decisions on the assumption that a dilemma exists.[4]

This is, I think, a straightforward challenge to the dominant view among whites, and especially white social scientists, that the values of American society would ultimately play a major role in overcoming the racial problem without resort to violence.

Another facet of the emergence of the black movement in the United States was signaled by Patrick Moynihan in his famous March, 1965, report, *The Negro Family.* He pointed out that the black revolution is related to what is going on in the rest of the world:

> It was not a matter of chance that the Negro movement caught fire in America at just that moment when the nations of Africa were gaining their freedom. Nor is it merely incidental that the world should have fastened its attention on events in the United States at a time when the possibility that the nations of the world will divide along color lines seems suddenly not only possible, but even imminent.[5]

A very strong statement about the direct link between Negro militancy and the outside world was made by J. Edgar Hoover before the House Appropriations Subcommittee on February 16, 1967. He said that Stokely Carmichael had been in frequent contact with Max Stanford, chairman of "a highly secret, all-

[4] Stokely Carmichael and Charles V. Hamilton, *Black Power, The Politics of Liberation in America* (New York: Random House–Vintage Books, 1967), p. 77.

[5] Daniel Patrick Moynihan, *The Negro Family—The Case for National Action* (Washington: United States Department of Labor, 1965), p. 1.

Negro, Marxist-Leninist, Chinese Communist-oriented organization which advocates guerilla warfare to obtain its goals."[6] This organization, called Revolutionary Action Movement (RAM), had 50 members according to the FBI.

In its August 5, 1966 issue the *Peking Review* mentioned the Revolutionary Action Movement in an article on the growing militancy of black Americans. It stated that RAM, "which has its headquarters in Philadelphia is now also active in New York, Chicago, Detroit, and other industrial centers in the north."[7] The same issue mentioned also the slogan "black power" which had just been launched by the Student Nonviolent Coordinating Committee.[8]

The following issue of the *Peking Review*[9] reproduced with great fanfare a statement made by Mao Tse-tung three years earlier on August 8, 1963, entitled *Statement Supporting the American Negroes in Their Just Struggle Against Racial Discrimination by U.S. Imperialism.* This, incidentally, was a unique document because Mao Tse-tung had not published anything under his signature for many years. The statement allegedly was written in response to a request from Robert Williams, a black American who had spent several years in Cuba and then moved to Peking. This document, both when it first was published and again when it was reproduced three years later, occasioned editorials in the Chinese press in which solidarity with the black nationalist movement was reaffirmed. It is quite understandable that the Chinese Communists would have seized upon a development of this sort and exploited it propagandistically, verbal support of national liberation movements being the only leverage the Chinese have nowadays in international politics.

But while the Chinese may be building this up out of proportion and may be harboring hopes that are perhaps excessive, it seems to me nevertheless dangerous to underestimate the role of leaders such as Stokely Carmichael and Rap Brown. I don't know enough about either to have a good feel for their political future, nor have I made any special effort to study their

[6] *Congressional Quarterly, op. cit.,* p. 1711.

[7] "Breaking the Fetters of 'Non-violence'," *Peking Review,* no. 32 (August 5, 1966), p. 29.

[8] *The New York Times,* "Excerpts from Paper on which the 'Black Power' Philosophy Is Based" (August 5, 1966), p. 10.

[9] *Peking Review,* no. 33 (August 12, 1966), pp. 12–13.

movements, but the Carmichael-Hamilton book is a sophisticated one, not the product of crude rabble rousers. The authors have done a lot of reading and thinking. Their rhetoric could hold its own against a Nkrumah or a Sukarno in their younger days when they started asserting themselves as nationalist leaders in their respective parts of the world. The literature of the black "liberation movement" deserves, I think, close attention.

Walter Williams has made the interesting observation that the blacks are moving from caste status to ethnic status, and that while in so doing they are taking new pride in themselves, they are also assimilating into the greater society.[10] But moving from caste status to ethnic status does not necessarily imply willingness to assimilate; it can also imply willingness to differentiate, to form a new and separate national entity rather than to merge into the dominant one.

There are indications that the black movement could go in a direction opposite from assimilation. St. Clair Drake, quoting Charles Silberman's *Crisis in Black and White,* points out how important the psychological effect of "powerlessness" is on the black community:

> Negroes realize that, as a minority in "the white man's country," they do not set the rules of the game. Unlike Negroes in Africa and the West Indies they do not fight for national independence, but rather for "desegration" and "integration," and they can attain these goals only if the white majority sanctions them as legitimate and desirable.[11]

It is obvious that the black movement in the United States, despite psychological similarities with national liberation movements in colonies, cannot become a full-fledged nationalist movement of the sort that has spread from Western Europe to the rest of the world since the beginning of the nineteenth century. First of all it represents not an oppressed majority against a colonialist minority but a permanent minority in an independent multiracial nation. Second, it cannot claim a terri-

[10] Walter Williams, "Power of Various Hues," unpublished paper prepared for the Rand Workshop on Urban Problems, December, 1967.

[11] St. Clair Drake, "The Social and Economic Status of the Negro in the United States," in Parsons and Clark, eds., *op. cit.*, pp. 35–36.

tory that could become the geographic base of an independent state. Seen in this light, black nationalism in the United States is bound to generate feelings of powerlessness, as none of the conventional goals of nationalism are capable of attainment.

But it would be misleading to judge the appeal of a movement only in terms of its practicality. What may appear as sheer sound and fury to an outsider may have strong emotional appeal for a member of the respective community.

Besides the feeling of helplessness engendered by the obvious lack of a true nationalist alternative, of a territory to be redeemed or liberated, one must also take into account in reflecting about the future of race relations in the United States the economic condition of the black population. Nathan Wright, the Plans Committee Chairman of the 1967 National Conference on Black Power, observes,

> when the so-called progress of the American Negro since World War II is viewed in its economic context, a strangely and perhaps frighteningly different kind of picture begins to appear. It is the kind of picture which gives a certain sense of logic to the increasing irrationality of the Negro's intensified and often angered protests.[12]

Dr. Wright uses official statistics to show here that median money income of families in the United States, in current dollars, grew as follows: the white population increased from $3,157 in 1947 to $6,548 in 1963, while the nonwhite population increased from $1,164 in 1947 to $3,465 in 1963.[13] The conclusions Dr. Wright draws from these figures are not that whereas the white incomes have doubled, the nonwhite incomes have trebled, but that the median income of nonwhites is still only half of the median income of the white population. He warns us that

> we are creating a monster within our midst, a people being alienated from the mainstream of American life, not by a deliberately malicious policy but by the sedation of ourselves into the feeling that things are not really as they are.[14]

[12] Nathan Wright, Jr., *Black Power and Urban Unrest* (New York: Hawthorn Books, Inc., 1967), p. 47.

[13] *Ibid.*, p. 48.

[14] *Ibid.*, p. 56.

Incidentally, Nathan Wright seems to be one of the moderate proponents of black power. He is associated with the National Committee of Negro Churchmen who discussed black power and had an advertisement in the *New York Times* on July 31, 1966, deploring "the overt violence of riots" although stating that "their basic causes lie in the silent and covert violence which white middle-class America inflicts upon the victims of the inner city."[15] Incidentally, in his book Dr. Wright never mentions Stokely Carmichael by name.

Thomas F. Pettigrew gives another relevant set of figures:

> If the rate of nonwhite gains between 1950 and 1960 continued, nonwhites would not attain equal proportional representation nationally among clerical workers until 1992, among skilled workers until 2005, among professionals until 2017, among sales workers until 2114, and among business managers and proprietors until 2730![16]

I submit that such figures go a long way in explaining the helplessness felt in the black community. This *is* very similar to what happens in a colonial situation. It is likely to help the militants in their appeal to the black population. Even if rates of change are speeded up, it may be too late to change psychological-political trends. When nationalist movements started taking hold in Asia and Africa, efforts by the colonial powers to introduce rapid reform were no longer useful, because they could do nothing fast enough to keep up with the rate of increase of militancy. The history of nationalist movements in the Third World has shown that there is a critical point at which reforms are no longer enough and a revolutionary situation has arisen.

But a nationalist-revolutionary movement is not necessarily a practical movement. History records hopeless situations. For instance, the Polish Jews before World War II are a tragic example. The Jews in Poland constituted just about the same percentage as the blacks in America today, about 10 percent. There were about three million of them. The predominant ideology they developed can most accurately be described as Jewish nationalism. They founded the Jewish Socialist Bund. It

[15] *Ibid.*, p. 188.

[16] Thomas F. Pettigrew, "Complexity and Change in American Racial Patterns: A Social Psychological View," in Parsons and Clark, eds., *op. cit.*, p. 332.

was an anti-Zionist socialist party that had a conception of the Jewish national identity. They weren't assimilationists; they wanted to speak Yiddish and maintain a separate Jewish culture. They called themselves nationalists, but they also wanted to separate themselves from the main current of Polish politics. There's a good descriptive history of the Jewish Bund, called the *Politics of Futility,* by Bernard K. Johnpoll.[17] The Polish Jews, like the black Americans, differed from other nationalists in that they had no majorities in any geographic area and could therefore not claim state power.

St. Clair Drake signals another phenomenon of major significance for the dynamics of nationalism:

> The Black Ghetto and the job ceiling . . . determine the crucial points of social reference for the individual Negro when answering the questions "who am I today?" and "what will I be tomorrow?" The Black Ghetto forces him to identify as a Negro first, an American second, and it gives him geographical "roots." The job ceiling is an ever present reminder that there are forces at work which make him a second-class American.[18]

If this statement is true, it provides an important argument in favor of the thesis that a process of differentiation of the black people from the rest of the American community may have set in, which may lead to an attempt to create a separate national entity, regardless of the irrationality of the whole endeavor.

Rupert Emerson, perhaps the most thoughtful contemporary student of nationalism, defines a nation as follows:

> The nation is today the largest community which, when the chips are down, effectively commands men's loyalty, overriding the claims both of the lesser communities within it and those which cut across it or potentially enfold it within a still greater society, reaching ultimately to mankind as a whole. In this sense the nation can be called a "terminal community" with the implication that it is for present purposes the effective end of the road for man as a social animal, the end point of working solidarity between men.[19]

[17] Bernard K. Johnpoll, *The Politics of Futility—The General Jewish Workers Bund of Poland, 1917–1943* (Ithaca: Cornell University Press, 1967).

[18] Drake, *op. cit.*, p. 32.

[19] Rupert Emerson, *From Empire to Nation—The Rise to Self-Assertion on Asian and African Peoples* (Cambridge, Mass.: Harvard University Press, 1960), pp. 95–96.

The obviously crucial question for us is: What is the terminal community for black Americans? Is it the black community itself, or is it the American nation? I don't know the answer, but I have no doubt that it is highly relevant. If it turned out to be that the black community is the terminal community, then the whole issue of whether the organization of black power is beneficial or not takes a very different aspect. Seymour Martin Lipset has said that black power might have a beneficial effect because it organizes people, it takes them out of the hands of the rabble rousers, and they then become forces for stability. But if they are organized on the basis of differentiation from the dominant community, this might create not stability but a socially explosive situation.

Before I comment on the next relevant statistics I would like to say a few more words about the dynamics of nationalism as explained by Karl W. Deutsch. He assumes that in a typically preindustrial society the majority of the population is passive or unmobilized politically. Social communication, aided by education and industrialization, at some point mobilizes this population, arousing its political consciousness. If an ethnically distinct population is mobilized before it is assimilated into the politically dominant population, then the process of differentiation tends to create a separate national entity.[20]

This is what happened in Central Europe in the period before World War I. The Czechs, the Slovaks, the Hungarians, and others became mobilized. They saw themselves as different from the Austrian, German-speaking, dominant population. They resented the dominance; they resented the fact that they could not express themselves in their own culture. Efforts to assimilate came too late. The result was that the Hapsburg Empire burst wide open, and separate nationalities were created. The same happens in Nigeria today. The same was about to happen in Indonesia in past years, but the Army was strong enough to keep it down. The same might still happen in India.

In this context one question to be answered is whether the black population in this country has really only become mobilized in the very recent past, these last few decades when the rural, passive, apathetic southern blacks moved North, entered industries, and went to high schools and colleges? And if so, is

[20] Karl W. Deutsch, *Nationalism and Social Communication—An Inquiry Into the Foundations of Nationality* (Cambridge, Mass.: Massachusetts Institute of Technology Press, 1953), Chap. VI.

it likely that the result will be similar to what happened in Central Europe, in Asia, and in Africa, namely the emergence of a distinct cultural identity, of a separate community, wanting a separate state? Again I don't know the answer.

Here are some interesting figures from the report that was circulated by the Los Angeles Riot Study (LARS) at U.C.L.A. The authors found in their two-year study in the Watts district that 30 percent of the blacks were militant, approving of the riots, in sympathy with the black power movement, believing that violence is doing the black community more good than harm; 35 percent were conservative, trying to advance within American society, wanting to do well by traditional devices and according to the values of this society; and 35 percent were uninvolved, passive. The breakdown of this sample in terms of employment is very interesting. Seventy percent of the militants and 63 percent of the conservatives were employed, as compared with 55 percent of the uninvolved.[21] This suggests that there is no direct correlation between radicalism and economic deprivation.

Of course, both the conservative group, representing the established "solid" black leadership, and the militant group are competing for the support of the passive group. The militants seem to be more successful[22] than the conservatives; the pull is toward the militant end of the spectrum as the passive, latent population begins to be mobilized. The U.C.L.A. study concludes:

> Essentially the "militants" are committed to a strategy of disrupting the system as a means of gaining greater bargaining power for helping the Negro move more rapidly into the economic and political streams. The social stream—integration—is no longer the primary goal. Integration becomes an individual goal rather than a group goal. What they are seeking is the right of any individual to have a choice. This is a long-range concern, however, and the power necessary to achieve it can be found through greater strength in the political and economic arenas. This in turn necessitates, at this

[21] Nathan E. Cohen, *The Los Angeles Riot Study,* mimeographed by the University of California, Los Angeles, Office of Public Information, August 1, 1967, p. 13.

[22] Nathan Glazer, "The Ghetto Crisis," *Encounter* (London) (November, 1967), p. 15.

time, the building up of a greater sense of identity, unity, and spirit of "nationalism."[23]

It seems to me that the belief that the conservative, middle-class, more successful black group will be able to restrain or outbid the militants and keep control of the black masses is predicated on certain notions that may not be realistic, judging from the experience of insurgencies or revolutionary movements in the Third World. For instance, in Algeria in the mid-1950s, a relatively small group of militants was able to intimidate the conservative, traditional leadership of the Arab community so effectively as to make them politically useless.[24]

I will not hazard a guess about how far the militants will go, if they achieve political control in the black community. Carmichael and Hamilton, writing in August 1967, described their book as presenting

> a political framework and ideology which represents the last reasonable opportunity for this society to work out its racial problems short of prolonged destructive guerrilla warfare. That such violent warfare may be unavoidable is not herein denied.[25]

Are the most radical militants simply putting us on? Or should we take the words of Carmichael, who has visited Havana, Algiers, and Hanoi, at face value? On July 25, 1967, according to the Havana radio, Carmichael stated in a press conference at the Habana Libre Hotel that he had established his first contact with the Cuban regime during the October, 1960, visit to New York of Fidel Castro.

If one ascribes any significant probability to the possibility that ghetto violence will escalate eventually into racial guerrilla warfare, then special attention must be devoted to the future attitudes of a crucial group in the black community, namely the veterans returning from the war in Vietnam. On June 21, 1967, the most recent date for which I was able to get

[23] Cohen, *op. cit.*, p. 17.

[24] William B. Quandt, *Revolution and Political Leadership—Algeria 1954–1968* (Cambridge, Mass.: Massachusetts Institute of Technology Press, 1969), Chap. VI.

[25] Carmichael and Hamilton, *op. cit.*, p. vi.

official figures, there were 44,500 black soldiers, including 1,000 officers, in Vietnam. They represented 10.6 percent of the total forces assigned to Vietnam, exactly proportional to the percentage of black citizens in the total population of the United States. But in terms of combat capability the black soldiers composed a significantly higher proportion of the total forces. Secretary of Defense Robert S. McNamara stated in a speech in Denver, Colorado, on November 7, 1967:

> It is a fact that Negroes often volunteer for the most difficult and hazardous assignments. It is a fact that 20 percent of Army deaths in Vietnam last year were Negroes.[26]

Not all black veterans of the Vietnam war will be thrown back into the ghetto. Officers and noncoms do not present a problem. Furthermore, many black soldiers reenlist. But the vast majority of black veterans return eventually to their own communities. There they face an entirely different situation from that experienced by the black veterans of previous wars, namely an increasingly mobilized social environment and constant exposure to radical agitators and organizers.

It is well established that people react more strongly against relative deprivation, the discrepancy between expectations and reality, than against habitual poverty. While I do not know anything about the state of mind of black veterans returning from Vietnam, I assume that being thrown back into the ghetto will be harder to take than it is for blacks who have never experienced equal treatment. Furthermore, combat veterans are bound to resent discrimination more keenly knowing that the community personally owes them a debt of gratitude. But most important, men who have lived through the intense experience of combat are likely to react more strongly than others to the idleness and want that may be in store for them after demobilization.

Everywhere in the world the returning veteran is potentially a political activist. If his personal needs, material as well as psychic, are satisfied, he is likely to become an active sup-

[26] Address by Robert S. McNamara, Secretary of Defense, at the National Association of Educational Broadcasters Forty-Third Convention (Washington, D.C.: Office of Assistant Secretary of Defense [Public Affairs], No. 1061–67), p. 7.

porter of his society. If frustrated, he is more prone to extremism than other, mentally less mobilized, individuals. For this reason it seems imperative to give full and urgent attention to the future social role of black veterans of the war in Vietnam. They are not simply returning to a frustrating environment but to one in which they will experience immediately extremist appeals.

Things have moved very fast since Stokely Carmichael and other members of the Student Nonviolent Coordinating Committee formulated the "black power" philosophy in August, 1966. At that time they proclaimed in rather restrained fashion that if "black people are not given their proper due and respect, then the antagonisms and contradictions are going to become more and more glaring, more and more intense, until a national explosion may result." A year later Stokely Carmichael advocated in Cuba "urban guerrilla warfare within the United States."[27]

If the notion of urban guerrilla warfare really takes hold among black radicals, obviously the black veteran, with recent combat experience in Vietnam, would become a principal target for political agitators and recruiters. Even if his loyalty as an American will protect him at first, the corrosive influence of protracted frustration cannot be minimized. Discrimination by itself might not have a strong enough impact to turn him into a terrorist, but aimless idleness and material and mental deprivations would, in time.

Some observers think that the danger of black terrorism is not a negligible one. Nathan Glazer has stated recently that the black militants are "indubitably the most radical movement in the country." They insist that "violence is natural and necessary, violence will come, and Negroes must be ready for it."[28] Judge Wade H. McCree, Jr., of the Sixth Circuit Court of Appeals told the National Conference of Christians and Jews that "the nation faces the threat of guerilla warfare fomented by 'Black Power' leaders, unless 'revolutionary' efforts are made to give Negroes full rights." He warned that

> 20 million people can make this country almost uninhabitable for a generation or more for the rest of the population and can create

[27] *Los Angeles Times*, December 12, 1967, quoting the Associated Press.

[28] Glazer, *op. cit.*, p. 17.

such chaos that the form of government which will ultimately emerge will bear scant resemblance to the one we venerate today.[29]

An even more disturbing warning came from the black newspaperman Carl T. Rowan, former USIA director and ambassador to Finland. In his nationally syndicated column, Rowan wrote that Detroit's leading black power organization, the Citywide Citizens Action Committee (CCAC), "has a larger following among the Negro masses of Detroit than any other group" and signaled "worrisome reports, backed by some evidence, that the Peking-oriented Progressive Labor Party is manipulating and perhaps financing CCAC through its Detroit operatives." Rowan also asserted that the President's Commission on Civil Disorders, in its Kerner Report, expressed concern that "CCAC has established increasing liaison with similar groups in other major cities, with the result that the black nationalists could have, in a few months, the most potent and effective political instrument among American Negroes."

Rowan also claimed in the same article that "the FBI and other intelligence sources have turned up 'pretty solid' evidence that Communist China used an elaborate international set of conduits to put a million dollars into Philadelphia[30] for use by the Revolutionary Action Movement. This is the group whose New York leaders were arrested on charges of plotting to kill NAACP and Urban League leaders Roy Wilkins and Whitney Young along with other civil rights 'moderates.' "

I strongly believe that special constructive measures for the benefit of black veterans of the war in Vietnam are urgently needed not only because justice demands it but also to counter the influence of the radicalized environment to which they will return in the ghetto. G.I. bill educational and housing benefits, available to all veterans, are not enough to change the life condition of school dropouts or to counter the forced segregation that keeps them in the ghetto. Obviously, the dangers facing American society cannot be eliminated by measures benefiting directly only less than 1 percent of the total black population. Only profound changes in the relationship between the white and black communities as a whole will really help.

[29] *Los Angeles Times,* December 14, 1967, quoting the Associated Press.

[30] Carl T. Rowan, "How to Avoid Guerilla Warfare," *Los Angeles Times,* December 6, 1967.

But students of nationalist and revolutionary movements are aware of the crucial importance of dedicated cadres. Measures that would deter black veterans from lending their skills and energy to extremism would be useful even though they would not provide a total solution.

Former Secretary McNamara was aware of this problem. In his November 7, 1967, speech to the National Association of Educational Broadcasters, he described briefly several Department of Defense efforts toward "the solution of the social problems wracking our nation." One of these is Project Transition. It is a voluntary program for men with 30 to 180 days of service time remaining. It consists of counseling, skill enhancement, education, and job placement. In early November, 1967, it was operative as a pilot program at five bases, but Mr. McNamara announced that "within sixty days Project Transition will be in operation at all eighty of the major installations in this country."[31] The Secretary of Defense stated that the Labor Department, DHEW, the Postal Service, and a number of state and local agencies that can assist with training and offer employment would cooperate, and that "the Ford Foundation has offered to work closely with us in solving the problems connected with placing the right veteran in the right job." While Mr. McNamara did not mention the danger of black veterans joining extremist movements, he did show special concern for this group:

> We are going to be able to give the returning Negro veteran—particularly the Negro veteran who without help might be compelled to drift back into the stagnation of the urban ghetto—an opportunity for valuable training and satisfying employment.

Maybe the Defense Department's Project Transition is sufficient to cope with the problems of returning black veterans. But in view of the potential danger represented by the fact that the war in Vietnam creates each year about 50,000 Negro veterans who could become the militarily trained cadres of a black terrorist movement, I prefer not to be complacent. The following questions merit serious attention.

1. What steps should be taken to allow black veterans who

[31] McNamara, *op. cit.*, p. 13.

may lack adequate educational background maximum benefits under the G.I. Bill of Rights?

2. How could black veterans be helped to take full advantage of federal assistance in purchasing a home?

3. What organizational arrangements could be devised to give black veterans special advantages in securing jobs in the private sector of the economy?

4. How could the proposal of the President's Commission on Technology, Automation, and Economic Progress that the Federal government become the "employer of last resort" (by hiring any man who can't get a job) be applied to black veterans?

5. What are the implications for black veterans and for the militant black movement of President Lyndon B. Johnson's appeal on November 15, 1967, to leaders of veterans' organizations to encourage more Vietnam veterans to become teachers, especially in poor ghetto, rural, and bordertown schools?

6. Can the November 21, 1967, memorandum of the Secretary of Defense authorizing early release from active duty of military men who are within 90 days of separation and wish to accept civilian police employment be used to associate black veterans with the law enforcement process, especially in the country's ghettos?

7. Professor James Q. Wilson of Harvard and Major Jerome Cavanagh of Detroit have proposed national riot-police forces. Should a special effort be made to use black veterans as an elite national riot-police force? Could such a body play a major role in temporarily arresting the danger of racial warfare in this country, thus gaining time for the major structural reforms required to reverse the present trend of alienation of black Americans?

The Role of News Media in the Urban Crisis

Ben H. Bagdikian

The Rand Corporation

It is said that in the 1920s the young men around President Hipolito Irigoyen in Argentina helped preserve the old man's peace of mind by printing a special edition of the leading Buenos Aires newspaper in the cellar of the presidential palace, replacing all disturbing news. If this story is true, it may have helped keep the President calm, but it didn't prevent subsequent turbulence in Argentina.

The United States has a good deal of bad news these days, and there is considerable blame placed on news media for provoking, or at least worsening, our ills. There is widespread feeling that newspapers and broadcasters are not just carriers of unpleasant information, but thrive on it, glorify it, and sometimes invent it. There is enough validity to the notion that the news media can create fashions in news to tempt us to try to cool contemporary urban events by cooling the news of them.

I would like to suggest that the opposite is true. The press has been guilty of carrying too little news about the urban crisis, not too much. When cities are in imminent danger of widespread guerilla warfare, it is no time to soothe the consumer with *Rebecca of Sunnybrook Farm.* This opinion, of course, depends on one's judgment of how bad the present urban situation is and the role of news media in it.

Regardless of how critical one believes the urban scene to be, or what its causes have been, the role of news media in the future is a powerful one and deserves attention. Before stating these, there ought to be some warnings that are obvious but worth repeating.

First, the urban crisis has an existence outside the news. The combination of racial revolution, poverty, and middle-class malaise produces disturbances where it is demonstrable that the news media have minimal effects, as in smaller cities where all media have agreed to quarantine provocative news. In the postwar South there were many communities where all media systematically screened out any civil rights news but nonetheless became the scene of civil rights crises.

Second, we are talking here of 1,750 daily papers and over 5,000 broadcasting stations. Many assumptions about "the press" are made by people who are really talking only about *The New York Times,* or the *Oakland Tribune,* or a disc jockey in Newark. These are relevant at varying times and places, but everyone—scholars, politicians, agitators, and journalists themselves—depends on impressions based on an extremely small sample of the news media. The author of this paper is no exception.

Third, some of the credit or blame for creating tides in reform and rebellion must be placed not on the news media but on the whole system of modern communications. The basic cause for rapid upheaval is an accelerated social reaction time all over the world, the faster propagation of ideas and their consequences. The press contributes to this. But even more important are contemporary patterns of affluence, education, travel, and communications outside the formal channels of news.

For example, the promise of the end of racial discrimination has been standard in the national political rhetoric for more than fifteen years, the promise of a large-scale attack on poverty, for almost eight years. This has been true of each President and of both major parties. Millions of poorly educated and politically unengaged citizens heard this rhetoric for the first time through television; and because so much of this rhetoric touched something basic in their lives, they tended to believe what this rhetoric said. Most of this was originally transmitted by the mass media outside the news channels. When the President of the United States wants to speak on these issues—as all presidents of the television era have wanted to—he has commanded prime time outside the news. When opponents in campaign time wanted to express themselves on these issues, they also were able to do it outside the news channels.

Nevertheless, the most systematic information does come from news channels, and these have hardly been perfect. Perhaps it helps to isolate the easy problems: fakery and carelessness. These are indefensible, and no professional tries to defend them, though some fakery and gross carelessness persist. Exposure almost always brings therapeutic results.

Much more difficult is the problem of "social responsibility" of news media when handling information that they believe is accurate but may have unpleasant social consequences, or may not be representative of an entire scene. These are the tough problems because they strike at a continuing dilemma of news media. The press is supposed to conceal nothing from the public, yet it is being asked on occasion to do it for the public's own good. It is being asked to display only "representative" news, yet if all the actors in the usual public event were brought together they would rarely agree on which of them was "representative." There is constant talk of judging news sources by their certifiable constituencies. Yet for all adjusting mechanisms—automated machines, fire departments, nation-states, bank bookkeepers—the most urgent information is evidence of a typical or irregular behavior. Should the news media alone be tied exclusively to reporting only authoritative, heavily supported voices? Especially when it cannot take the time to wait for the judgment of history? How many of us truly want news editors to exercise that standard of judgment on all matters?

These issues are important in more than academic ways, both to preserve independence in the press and to avoid uniform error. I would like to suggest a general strategy by which our media preserve their openness and their commitment. It helps to see that American journalism is not a monolithic process but perhaps five different ones that are collectively purposeful but have protections against the dangers of a closed system.

The first step in news is deciding what to focus on. We are

guided by conventions of what constitutes news. If the media are really good, they give high priority to what will influence public affairs. So far we have been relatively insensitive to signs of social dislocation. We have depended too much on social explosion as a symptom of social trouble. The gathering storm of race and poverty was in the statistics for at least 20 years, but journalism's early warning system was crude. What we need in journalism is men in touch with scholarship and social action, for the initial purpose not just to report physical drama but for detecting signs that our system is maladjusted. In a fast-moving, dynamic society, it is an increasingly important role of the press. After practice and policy are established, it may be too late.

Once we have decided where to turn our cameras and reporters, objective reporting of the scene is fairly good. We still have some faking of happenings, mostly by broadcasters, but they are discovering, as the printed press did earlier, that this catches up with you. Distortion of observed events is the unforgivable contamination of the whole process of information. In general, conventional reporting works fairly well.

Once we have focused and described a scene, we may have confronted the citizen with a need to make a decision. This is certainly true in poverty and race. Everyone who looks at television or reads a newspaper understands instinctively that things are never going to be the same again in this country. The straight news says that. Everyone has to move. But where? What are the choices? Where is intelligent self-interest? Here we may be creating a social explosion, impelling people out of the status quo without giving them information on where to go.

But this is also our philosophical problem. Who are we to point at the pathway? The Constitution did not visit upon the press Divine Wisdom, only the right to make mistakes.

Here, I think, there are three different steps that help us solve the problem. The first is to be less fearful of the free marketplace of ideas. We need to open the news system to complainers in order to propel grievances into the public consciousness. We need to report promoters of radical ideas in order to raise consideration of basic change and test current orthodoxies. We are not defenseless against the charlatan and the crank, but we need to be broad rather than narrow.

I disagree with those who would deny Rap Brown and

Stokely Carmichael access to the news system simply because they are inflammatory and feed on publicity. History warns us to be wary of deciding ahead of time what will stimulate utilitarian answers. I remember that in the 1940s we were told not to report the demonstrations sponsored by Roy Wilkins and the NAACP because they did not represent the mass of Negroes, that for every person signing a petition or walking a picket line there were 1,000 on the opposite side. This was said about Thurgood Marshall's endless string of court actions in the 1950s, then of James Farmer, then of Robert Moses, then of Malcolm X. Many of the same editors and some of the same government officials who bitterly opposed the reporting of activities and speeches of Wilkins and Marshall are today bitter because race reporting does not concentrate solely on those same men. The reverberations caused by activists are important, and the news media cannot wait to see if events evolve without publicity. It is safer to report what seems to make an impact, even if it is confused with the impact of the news mechanism itself.

If we stopped there we would depend excessively on noise and drama. We don't need to. News media on their own should seek out thoughtful people with rational ideas on problems, even if these ideas differ from the medium's. These ideas should be presented fairly and clearly as a contribution to the public reservoir of possible solutions. Here again we need journalists at home in the field of scholarship, of social action, and of ideas, who know where to turn, and who support the philosophy of tolerance of differing views. And we need proprietors who encourage this.

Finally, there is the medium's own recommendation, its editorials. It is fashionable to dismiss editorials as completely meaningless. I think this is a mistake. It is true that editorials don't get their way in their most noticeable commitments, such as endorsements for President of the United States. Historically, and especially in the last generation, papers have been notoriously unsuccessful in this, except for 1964. It is also true that their impact on the average reader is not very clear. But especially on local issues, and on national issues where social and economic values are concerned, editorials tend to set the limits of permissible debate in the community. While this has to be conjecture, it is worth considering how important such editorial values have been in the perpetuation of the national pieties that all public sector spending is inherently bad, all planning dangerous, and all economic activity that is not predicated on a simple market economy is subversive. This has special meaning in the urban crisis. Most metropolitan papers in cities that have gone through the agony of ghetto violence now report the ghetto with more perception and seriousness than before. Often their description of causes is good. But almost without exception, the obvious remedies—some kind of large-scale action to reform the ghetto school, improve housing, increase municipal services, discover a nondestructive substitute for welfare, and provide practical employment—find the conservative conventions of most American editorial pages unable to make such remedies a standard item in respectable debate in the most influential circles of the American community.

In the crisis of the cities there has been insufficient national identification of basic solutions. Because politics adjusts to the communications system, some of this can be laid to the door of a press that, editorially, is wedded to a nostalgic and simplistic view of the economy. It took the president of the Ford Motor Company to make the negative income tax a respectable subject of debate in public.

There are powerful reasons for the news media's doing all of these things. They may spell the difference between success and failure in negotiating rapid social change. Margaret Mead has described how some Pacific tribes in one generation successfully changed cultures that had been stable for a thousand. The key was to keep all elements in touch with each other. Otherwise, the older, more conservative echelons in the rear become anxious from the mysterious happenings up front and hold back, clinging to the familiar. The younger, aggressive generation up front interprets this as sabotage from the rear. The result is anarchy and civil war. I can think of some contemporary parallels.

The news media have peculiar strengths as common carriers during a time of change. In this country, we don't have exclusive channels of information to separate audiences, at least not yet. We all have the same chance to glimpse what the media say is reality. In fact, it's almost the only common source of contact left in a society increasingly segregated not only by race but also by age, income, and education. Yet what the mass media tell these separate audiences about the human qualities of their unseen fellow citizens is pretty depressing when you realize that social values are shaped not just when an announcer puts on a long face or the headline implies, "We are now going to be serious." The national values also arise from entertainment and advertising.

Before deciding on details of policy I think we ought to face a basic failing: When it comes to race and poverty we don't know our subjects very well. If there is one thing the local newspaper and broadcaster are sure of, it's that they know their own community. I've spent some time among the rural and ghetto poor over the last ten years; and I'm afraid that, when it comes to the poor, that just isn't true. Very few local news organizations know much about poverty and nonwhite life, though they usually think they do. I learned very early that you get one picture if you look at the ghetto from outside and above, a completely different one if you begin inside and at the bottom. That's why it's a ghetto: it doesn't connect well with the outside.

The answer isn't just to hire Negro reporters. It requires someone, black or white, who is competent and able to cross cultural lines naturally. I think the most efficient way to understand the ghetto is to live in it a few days, not as a stunt nor just out of sympathy or sentimentality. If I were a city editor or a news director, I would certainly require this of any reporter specializing in poverty and the ghetto. It's remarkable how otherwise incomprehensible events and emotions become clear after you have spent some time in the everyday existence of this strange island in our national life. We ourselves need better knowledge of what we're reporting.

Then we need to be more explicit about causes and about remedies. We need to learn how to write clearly and well about them, putting them in human terms. Broadcasting documentaries and magazines have done this well, newspapers less so. By telling everyone, black and white, that their lives are going to change, we create explosions unless we can describe believable pathways of change.

I'd like to conclude with a word on prevention of riots or of unnecessary triggering of riots by the mass media. The outbreak or the imminence of outbreak means that already the system has failed, but this doesn't relieve the media of their responsibilities to act wisely during crisis. I appreciate this fact, and yet I have seen some guidelines for local media policy during racial crisis that strike me as dangerous. A number of these declare that either no news of a certain kind will be given out, or that the news will always stress the constructive, or the media commit themselves to give out only what the authorities give out, such as not calling an outbreak a riot until the police and the mayor call it a riot.

Precisely because a riot or near-riot is so frightening there is the danger of rumor, panic, and paranoia. Panic and paranoia can destroy us faster than civil disorder accelerated by the mass media. If large segments of our population lose confidence in their formal systems of information, they will invent their own. Our talk about race relations constitutes the only measure the ghetto-dweller has of how much he can trust our accuracy. If in the things he knows best, the news is false or inaccurate, he may later be unreachable in more fundamental ways.

I recognize that there are times when delay is justified, but these should be limited, imposed with an awareness that concealment and delay are costly medicine. Deception in the news and a degree of delay that amounts to deception leads to public paranoia and to demoralization of the news system; therefore, three principles ought to govern the reporting of civil disorder: The first is, "Never lie"; the second is "Never lie"; and the third is, "Never lie."

We need to realize something else quite practical. The mass media are the most pervasive formal channel of communication in the ghetto, but not the only source of information. Ghetto news is passed mainly by word-of-mouth. This includes telephone. When there are gunfire and flames around an apartment house, most of the tenants are on the phone telling relatives and friends. Then all of them may hear a broadcast report that all is quiet.

The more highly organized the ghetto, the more likely it is that a separate network of information may displace the mass media as a believable source. For example, I have talked to a group in Watts that regularly monitors police band radio. You can buy a complete portable receiver for police and fire calls for $25. For $10 you can buy a preset police call receiver attachable to any portable transistor radio. For $2.95 in any radio shack you can buy a book of police broadcast codes. The group I talked to in Watts had all of these plus two-way radios in cars. They were what I would call moderates among activists in the ghetto. Their purpose was to beat the police to a call and stand at the scene taking Polaroid flash shots and tape recordings of police handling of an arrest. They claimed that it had a noticeable effect on treatment of suspects. But it also gave them a very accurate fix on what was going on in potential civil disorder throughout the area. These people had well-organized communications lines to the whole ghetto community. We have a greater stake in maintaining belief in the accuracy and honesty of our news media than we do in avoidance of disturbing news.

Lastly we need to remember that manipulation of news can further distort public decision-making on a subject already suffering from inadequate awareness at every level of society of the realities of our crisis.

Index

Selected Rand Books

Becker, Abraham. *Soviet National Income, 1958–1964: The National Accounts of the USSR in the Seven Year Plan Period.* University of California Press, Berkeley and Los Angeles, California, 1969.

Bergson, Abram. *The Real National Income of Soviet Russia Since 1928.* Harvard University Press, Cambridge, Massachusetts, 1961.

——— and Hans Heymann, Jr. *Soviet National Income and Product, 1940–48.* Columbia University Press, New York, New York, 1954.

Chapman, Janet G. *Real Wages in Soviet Russia Since 1928.* Harvard University Press, Cambridge, Massachusetts, 1963.

Downs, Anthony. *Inside Bureaucracy.* Little, Brown and Company, Boston, Massachusetts, 1967.

Goldhamer, Herbert and Andrew W. Marshall. *Psychosis and Civilization.* The Free Press, Glencoe, Illinois, 1953.

Hirshleifer, Jack, James C. DeHaven, and Jerome W. Milliman. *Water Supply: Economics, Technology, and Policy.* The University of Chicago Press, Chicago, Illinois, 1960.

Hitch, Charles J. and Roland N. McKean. *The Economics of Defense in the Nuclear Age.* Harvard University Press, Cambridge, Massachusetts, 1960.

Hoeffding, Oleg. *Soviet National Income and Product in 1928.* Columbia University Press, New York, New York, 1954.

Johnson, William A. *The Steel Industry of India.* Harvard University Press, Cambridge, Massachusetts, 1966.

Kershaw, Joseph A. and Roland N. McKean. *Teacher Shortages and*

Salary Schedules. McGraw-Hill Book Company, Inc., New York, New York, 1962.

Liu, Ta-Chung and Kung-Chia Yeh. *The Economy of the Chinese Mainland: National Income and Economic Development, 1933–1959.* Princeton University Press, Princeton, New Jersey, 1965.

Lubell, Harold. *Middle East Oil Crises and Western Europe's Energy Supplies.* The Johns Hopkins Press, Baltimore, Maryland, 1963.

Marschak, Thomas, Thomas K. Glennan, Jr., and Robert Summers. *Strategy for R&D.* Springer-Verlag New York Inc., New York, New York, 1967.

McKean, Roland N. *Efficiency in Government Through Systems Analysis: With Emphasis on Water Resource Development.* John Wiley & Sons, Inc., New York, New York, 1958.

Mead, Margaret. *Soviet Attitudes Toward Authority: An Interdisciplinary Approach to Problems of Soviet Character.* McGraw-Hill Book Company, Inc., New York, New York, 1951.

Meyer, John R., Martin Wohl, and John F. Kain. *The Urban Transportation Problem.* Harvard University Press, Cambridge, Massachusetts, 1965.

Moorsteen, Richard. *Prices and Production of Machinery in the Soviet Union, 1928–1958.* Harvard University Press, Cambridge, Massachusetts, 1962.

Nelson, Richard R., Merton J. Peck, and Edward D. Kalachek. *Technology, Economic Growth and Public Policy.* The Brookings Institution, Washington, D.C., 1967.

Rosen, George. *Democracy and Economic Change in India.* University of California Press, Berkeley and Los Angeles, California, 1966.

Williams, J. D. *The Compleat Strategyst: Being a Primer on the Theory of Games of Strategy.* McGraw-Hill Book Company, Inc., New York, New York, 1954.

Wolf, Charles, Jr. *Foreign Aid: Theory and Practice in Southern Asia.* Princeton University Press, Princeton, New Jersey, 1960.